Joy,
Inspiration,
and Hope

Number One

CAROLYN AND ERNEST FAY SERIES
IN ANALYTICAL PSYCHOLOGY
David H. Rosen, General Editor

Joy,
Inspiration,
and Hope

Verena Kast

TRANSLATED BY DOUGLAS WHITCHER

FOREWORD BY DAVID H. ROSEN

Texas A&M University Press
College Station

The paper used in this book meets the minimum requirements
of the American National Standard for Permanence
of Paper for Printed Library Materials, Z39.48-1984.
Binding materials have been chosen for durability.

LIBRARY OF CONGRESS CATALOGING-IN-PUBLICATION DATA

Kast, Verena, 1943–
    Joy, inspiration, and hope / Verena Kast ; translated by
Douglas Whitcher ; foreword by David H. Rosen. — 1st ed.
        p.   cm. — (Carolyn and Ernest Fay series in ana-
lytical psychology; no. 1)
    Includes bibliographical references and index.
    ISBN 0-89096-470-X
    1. Joy.   2. Inspiration.   3. Hope.   I. Title.   II. Series.
BF575.H27K37   1991
152.4 — dc20   90-47362
                                                        CIP

Number One
CAROLYN AND ERNEST FAY SERIES
IN ANALYTICAL PSYCHOLOGY
David H. Rosen, General Editor

The Carolyn and Ernest Fay edited book series, based initially on the annual Fay Lecture Series in Analytical Psychology, was established to further the ideas of C. G. Jung among students, faculty, therapists, and other citizens and to enhance scholarly activities related to analytical psychology. The Book Series and Lecture Series address topics of importance to the individual and to society. Both series were generously endowed by Carolyn Grant Fay, the founding president of the C. G. Jung Educational Center in Houston, Texas. The series are in part a memorial to her late husband, Ernest Bel Fay. Carolyn Fay has planted a Jungian tree carrying both her name and that of her late husband, which will bear fruitful ideas and stimulate creative works from this time forward. Texas A&M University and all those who come in contact with the growing Fay Jungian tree are extremely grateful to Carolyn Grant Fay for what she has done. The holder of the Frank N. McMillan, Jr. Professorship in Analytical Psychology at Texas A&M functions as the general editor of the Fay Book Series.

Contents

viii

Part V. **Hope**

Foreword

VERENA KAST GREW UP in a farming village in Switzerland. I imagine her as a basically happy, animated, and optimistic child playing, singing, and being in contact with the earth and its animals, herbs, and flowers. I sense this to be true after meeting her, hearing her lectures, and reading this book. It seems that she has liberated her inner child and those wondrous, but all too often neglected, emotions of joy, inspiration, and hope. Verena infects you with her mirth, enthusiasm, and assurance. It makes perfect sense that before her career in psychology, she was a school teacher in a small rural Swiss town.

When I first talked with Professor Kast in Zurich (June, 1989) about being the inaugural Fay Lecturer, she was very pleased to learn that Texas A&M University had a history of being tied to the land. I asked Verena what the theme would be for her lecture series in the spring of 1990, and she replied, "I want to lecture on emotions that we do not usually focus on." I inquired further, and she gave the following as the title of her lecture series: "Joy, Inspiration, Hope, and the Individuation Process." I was excited, because it is true that we do not ordinarily concentrate on such topics, especially in a scholarly way.

Unknowingly, at that time Verena was also being prophetic. Now we all feel the joy of the newfound freedom in Eastern Europe; we share the inspiration that comes from casting off the oppression of totalitarianism, and we all experience a renewed sense of hope as walls have come tumbling down and people embrace one another. Individuation, which Jung first described in individuals and has to do with the process of moving toward wholeness, is now also occurring on national and regional levels. There is a concept called synchronicity in Jungian psychology that is related to meaningful precognition and/or simultaneous coincidences. The psychological phenomena are related to acausal connections and find a parallel in modern quantum physics. It seems as though Verena has tapped into something related to synchronicity, something of immense importance for all of us. Perhaps it suggests that the decade of the 1990s will be a transitional one heralding a new millennium in which there will be true "peace on earth"; a time when we shall all be conscious members of one human family. At least, we can hope that this is the direction in which we are evolving.

William James, the founder of both American psychology and American philosophy, stated, "Human beings can alter their lives by altering their attitudes of mind." Dr. Kast extends this view to include the unattended to but essential emotions of joy, inspiration, and hope. We can change our lives by acknowledging and experiencing these unheeded feelings.

Professor Kast's book is thoughtful, provocative, as well as practical. It is also inspirational and renews one's faith and hope in "the human being as a creature of joy." Dr. Kast's writing has creative vitality, and one can sense her delight throughout the book. It exudes a feeling of trust and emits hope that can only facilitate one's individuation process.

Etymologically, psychology means the study of the soul — that is, that enlightening spirit or life-giving force which gives rise to those stabilizing, integrating powers that make a being whole and a person fully human. Such a person can find meaning and purpose in life and can feel optimism, sensitivity, receptivity, empathy, and creativity. But we have neglected three basic emotions that relate to the soul. It is of these emotions that Dr. Kast writes. She points out that we research and concentrate on the dark side — depression, sorrow, and despair. But she emphasizes the need to explore the bright and light side — the world of the carefree child. She offers an anatomy of joy that deals with intrapsychic and interpersonal joy and its sources. Professor Kast outlines a practical way to contact joy that has been buried since childhood; she calls this technique the "biographical reconstructions of joy." She shows us how to use this technique to reexperience our repressed joys from childhood and to bring these emotions into consciousness.

The next part of the book concerns inspiration, the opposite of expiration or death. Inspiration is synonymous with life, and that is the basic issue. Are we going to live or die? *"To be or Not to be?"* Inspiration is on the side of *"To be."* It implies that we have purpose, that we are moving toward something, and that we have direction and meaning in our lives or we are pursuing the quest. This part also deals with ecstasy and creativity and how they relate to inspiration.

In the final part of the book, Dr. Kast focuses on hope, which is also related to life, the future, and "To be." It is the opposite of hopelessness and *"Not to be."* What a therapeutic agent hope is! Dr. Kast not only spotlights this unsung and uncared for emotion, but she suggests ways to encourage its development and bring it into consciousness. She prescribes a rekindling of the flame of personal hope and embeds it finally in the context of *absolute hope*, something akin to faith.

Dr. Kast's writing is inspirational, hopeful, creative, and transformative. For the most part, this book focuses on the individual and one's own psychic growth. However, Dr. Kast suggests that as the person individuates (engages in a process toward wholeness), relationships and groups beyond the individual will be influenced and vice versa. In other words, the concepts in this book can be extended to families, communities, societies, and Mother Earth. Verena Kast uproots and then bridges, by joining areas well known in psychology with areas that are less known, unfamiliar, and underdeveloped. It seems that psychology (and most of us) deviated off the right path and apparently got lost along the way, reminiscent of Dante's quote:

> In the middle of the journey of our life
> I found myself in a dark wood,
> For I had lost the right path.

Are we now experiencing psychology's (and our) midlife crisis? A symptom of this wrong turn is the concentration by psychology and our society on anxiety, conflict, violence, despair, demoralization, meaninglessness, and hopelessness. Dr. Kast's book brings psychology and us back onto the right path — through joy, inspiration, and hope — toward wholeness, individuation, and the actualization of our potential.

On the cover of this book is a moonflower drawn by John Walker, an artist and professor of architecture at Texas A&M University. The moonflower is very pertinent in a symbolic way to the essence of Dr. Kast's book. The moonflower is a tropical, night-blooming morning glory (*Calonyction aculeatum*) with fragrant white or purple flowers. The two parts of the name moonflower are significant. The moon is dark and feminine, but it is light as it reflects the sun (masculine), so it is an androgynous entity, a Yin/Yang symbol. The fact that the moonflower only blooms at night means that out of the darkness comes creative blossoming. Flower means the best of the emotions; and joy, inspiration, and hope surely are choice natural and positive emotions that emerge out of the darkness. It is a paradox. When there is demoralization in the psyche, society, and the land, there is despair, meaninglessness, and hopelessness, a living deadness. But just on the other side is the blossom, the restoration of morale, delight, meaning, and hope; a symbolic death and new life. The moonflower is an edifying symbol for the cover of this breakthrough work. It represents the Soul and the idea that out of the darkness emerge the creative emotions of joy, inspiration, and hope.

William Wordsworth held the view that the soul of the human being had at its very core a deep relationship with the forces at work in the world of essential nature and that those forces in the last analysis represented joy. Regarding inspiration, Ovid said, "There is a deity within us, who breathes that divine fire by which we are animated." Emily Dickinson wrote,

> Hope is the thing with feathers
> That perches in the soul,
> And sings the tune without the words,
> And never stops at all.

Verena Kast has written a book that embodies what Wordsworth, Ovid, and Dickinson expressed. She has something very special. In Africa it is called *obuntu, botho*, which Archbishop Desmond Tutu defines as: "The essence of being human. You know when it is there, and when it is absent. It speaks about humaneness, gentleness, putting yourself out on behalf of others, being vulnerable. It embraces compassion and toughness. It recognizes that my humanity is bound up in yours, for we can only be human together."

DAVID H. ROSEN

College Station, Texas

Acknowledgments

I WOULD LIKE TO EXPRESS my most sincere thanks to Carolyn Fay and the late Ernest Fay, who have made the Fay Lectures in Analytical Psychology—and their publication in a book series —possible and who awarded me with the great honor of opening them in 1990. I hope that this fine idea will spark much intellectual stimulation and inspiration. I would also like to express warm appreciation to Professor David Rosen of Texas A&M University, who not only took on the demanding task of organizing the Fay Lectures and but who also acted as my kind host during my rewarding visit to Texas A&M and as an attentive colleague during the publication of the text. I thank Douglas Whitcher for the enthusiasm, empathy, and competence with which he converted verbatim transcripts of my German lectures into a written English text. Thanks are also due to Elizabeth Burr, who was consulted on the translation and skillfully edited it.

Joy,
Inspiration,
and Hope

Prologue

IT IS ASTONISHING how little has been written about joy, inspiration, and hope — the emotions of elation — in the field of psychology, especially depth psychology. The emotions of anxiety, grief, and rage have been investigated much more thoroughly, with anxiety assuming a position of such importance that it practically seems to define a vision of the human being as a whole. Naturally we are aware that the emotions of elation exist alongside those of depression — indeed we long for joy, states of inspiration, and hope.

But we are ambivalent: we both seek after these emotions and hold them suspect. If we see someone in a joyful state who is perhaps a bit boisterous, suspicions are quickly raised in our minds about whether we may be witnessing the repression of some problem. On the other hand, if someone is depressed or in a dark mood, it hardly occurs to us to ask if this is a case of repressed joy. If we consent to what psychology, especially depth psychology, has had to say about the elated emotions, it is difficult to avoid the view that a mature human being on the path of individuation will be predominantly serious, and that the goal of the individuation process might even be to live the remainder of our lives in tragic resignation, conscious of darkness and difficulty, while dismissing the lighter, happier side of life.

4

My concern in this book is to explore how the elated emotions can function in the process of individuation and to propose a view of the human being as a creature of joy, complementing the already familiar view of the human being as a creature of anxiety. Whereas anxiety drives the individual into isolation, joy is the foundation of alliance and solidarity. Human beings are both anxious and joyful by nature; we need both solitude and relationship. Individuation requires both parts.

In therapy, we therapists endeavor to strengthen self-esteem. Joy is a strengthening resource that life naturally offers, so it seems meaningful to draw on joy as part of our classic efforts at strengthening the ego complex. We need only think of what can happen when we fall in love to imagine the transformative potential of joy. This book's therapeutic aim is to seek out ways to stimulate and enlarge both the joys that we have already experienced and those that are potentially ours. It is my view that transformation is possible not only when we endure our deepest anxieties and fathom the depths of despair, but also when we experience the full range of joy.

Why, then, are the elated emotions so often disparaged as childish or dismissed as the expressions of naive and tender-minded souls? Emotions in general do not enjoy a good reputation, and the elated emotions in particular are held in question and, indeed, suspicion. I will attempt to allay some of the anxieties that arise in connection with elated emotions. I will also argue that a psychology of emotions must be biographical, based on a position of existential involvement.

Thus I will be inviting you to reconstruct your own biography of joy in order to reflect with me on the nature and function of joy in our lives. And I will show by example how this method of investigating the emotion of joy can give us insights into the personality not otherwise attainable. I believe that analysts can fruitfully incorporate this approach into their work.

I came to this approach when a seriously depressed woman with suicidal tendencies moved me to help her reconstruct her biography of joy in the course of her therapy. In the process, she recalled sources of joy from her childhood which had been lost through events that were only briefly mentioned in her usual case history. She then realized how she had unconsciously attempted to recreate these early joys in a narcissistic fashion later in life and how she had repressed her joy. As she began to re-experience joy, she found a growing wholeness for her life.

By comparing reconstructed biographies of joy gathered from a number of individuals in various life situations, I can go on to sketch a preliminary anatomy of joy. What creates joy and what spoils it? What are the varieties of joy? How is joy developed in memory? What is the nature of the joy of looking forward to something? Why is uninhibited joy something we generally restrict to children? What is the role of joy in the development of the personality? What are the shadow sides of joy? In the background of this anatomy of joy we will hear the persistent question, Can joy be induced?

Then I move to an examination of the elated emotions of inspiration and ecstasy, taking the existential view of mania provided by Kretschmer and Binswanger as my point of departure. Mania represents the elated half of a "circular madness" that alternates between extremes of joy and sadness. Mania's constituents of heightened drive, elevated mood, and flight of ideas seem to correspond to a deep contemporary longing to be carried up into the heights. Fasting, meditation, intoxication, and drugs are all ways by which we aspire to the experience of transcendence, if only for a brief moment. Elated emotional states make us feel connected to other persons, to our inner world, perhaps even to the cosmos. Whether this seductive feeling leads in the end to festive joy and creativity or to a manic repression of depression, depends on whether we are able to maintain what

Binswanger called "the human balance" between the vertical and horizontal dimensions of being. We must let ourselves be seized, but then we must also actualize in concrete reality what we have experienced when we were soaring in the heights. Binswanger observed that if we do not maintain this balance we may become "high-flown." However, if we do ground ourselves, the door is opened to creativity.

Inspiration has been explained from ancient times as the effect of divine activity, and ecstasy as the action of a human being stepping outside himself or herself to make room for a god. The story of Pentecost, in which the Holy Spirit seizes the disciples, illustrates the experiences of inspiration, ecstasy, and intoxication. From a psychological point of view, inspiration and ecstasy occur when the unconscious is activated and ego boundaries become highly permeable. In this state, connection with other persons at the level of the unconscious is intensified. Thus the social embeddedness or ritual arrangement of inspiration and ecstasy is very important. Because we live in a time that is poor in living religious rituals, we tend to privatize them, with the result that they can be genuinely deadly—for example, in the solitary alcoholic.

The Greek god Dionysus can be seen as a symbolic expression of the cluster of emotions that includes enthusiasm, inspiration, intoxication, and ecstasy, on the verge of becoming hope. Those seized by Dionysus broke out of the conventional order to become part of a cosmic order; human beings became one with nature, social rank was obliterated, rivalries ceased. Torn out of their isolation, individuals experienced prophecy and a momentary connection with the transpersonal Self. If we wish to pursue the question how human beings can be more powerfully united, we need to consider what kinds of life experiences can bring us into contact with a suprapersonal Self.

Hope is the foundation for creativity, inspiration, joy, and all those emotions which allow us to transcend ourselves. I turn last to hope. Albert Camus saw in Sisyphus an absurd hero who achieved happiness without hoping. French existentialism waged a campaign against hope, unleashing a controversy that pitted hope as a "fatal evasion" against hope as the basis for a sense of safety, security, and confidence in life. In spite of the existentialist quest to avoid all forms of hope, a hidden hint of hope can be perceived in the figure of Sisyphus himself, who expected the gods to lose their nerve in the face of his Stoic resolve. Camus's and Sartre's battles against decadent forms of optimism, rather than eliminating every responsible notion of hope, clear the way for a radical concept of absolute hope.

In this context, I construct a continuum of anticipation that ranges from rigid expectation at one end, to hope independent of any specific content at the other. Then I develop a view of hope that combines Erikson's basic trust, Bloch's not-yet-conscious hope, and Jung's anticipatory healing nature of the psyche. Marcel maintained that this form of hope is akin to faith.

Even though hope represents the basic emotional confidence that underlies all other feelings of elation, I propose that therapeutic work should begin at the level of joy. If we can relearn to be joyful and to admit joy into our lives, we will also gain consciousness of the somewhat abstract, elemental feeling of hope, which will then in turn become an increasingly sustaining foundation of our existence.

In the foreground of joy stands the identity of ego with the transpersonal Self, a convergence that enlarges the experience of the ego and enables it to open up and experience something unexpected. In the background is the archetype of the divine child, who dwells in the fullness of the positive mother archetype. By means of the elated emotions, which involve us more closely in symbiosis, we experience fullness of being, vitality, and connectedness with other persons; we experience the Self through momentary forgetfulness of self. This seems to me to represent an important modification of classical Jungian understandings of the concept of individuation. The elated emotions evoke an aspect of the human being that calls for study and reflection. But in order to be able to think about the elated emotions, we must first address the role that emotions play in human life as a whole.

PART I

A Psychology of the Emotions

I.

The Foolishness of the Tender-minded?

As I EMBARK ON THE TASK of speaking and writing about joy, inspiration, and hope, I find that I am a bit excited and that I get a mischievous pleasure out of exploring a topic that has received such scant attention in the field of psychology. Now I have told you what sort of mood I am in. What sort of mood are you in? This is not such a simple question, as we will see.

But why a psychology of emotions in the first place? Why, in spite of all the trends and publications in cognitive psychology, does it remain so important? In general terms, a psychology of emotions is important because when we work with emotions we are working with our identity. When I said I feel mischievous pleasure in writing this book, by implication I revealed something of myself. When we speak of emotions, we speak of ourselves. When we perceive an emotion, we experience ourselves.

Moreover, an emotion always has to do with existential involvement. An attempt to eliminate emotions would result in persons who no longer permitted themselves to be involved with life. To stop letting ourselves be involved in this way means to stop feeling, to stop caring, to stop acting. When we see something horrible without permitting ourselves to get involved, we turn our backs and walk away. If we do not get involved, we do not act.

But have no fear that I am going to subsume emotion under the heading of action. In the past few years, there have been various attempts to place emotion in the service of action. This is an important aspect of the subject. If we are not involved—do not feel—we do not act, because we have no energy to act. This is why many forms of therapy repeatedly emphasize getting in touch with the emotions. Emotions generate the energy to make needed changes, to take needed actions.

However, emotions also have their own value apart from what they lead to. For example, I think it is important to be able to experience joy with each other without having to become friends immediately. Joy may result in alliance, but being delighted may also be simply a state of the ego. I can say, "I'm delighted," independent of any "which means that. . . ." Emotion is the way we experience ourselves. When we speak of emotions, we speak of ourselves personally, we take ourselves seriously. And we take others seriously when we listen to their emotions. It is a matter of our experience of identity.

Emotions always involve the body, too. If you are very joyful, you will sense it physically. If I say, "My pulse is racing; maybe it is from excitement or joy," this is a physical perception. Our facial expression is a related aspect of emotions and their perception which we cannot leave out of consideration. We are used to distinguishing various emotions from each other, even if we do not verbalize the differences. We do this by means of the body, and as we know, "The body doesn't lie." I may say, "I am happy," and then make the face of a death mask. You will probably believe my face and disregard my words. Or I may be unsuccessful in my attempt to keep my joy under control, and so I laugh. Without words, I will have told you of my happiness.

Emotions concern who we are as persons, our experience of identity, and our involvement. My body plays its part, and my body and I interact within a social environment. We share something about ourselves through our emotions; we give each other signals. What we call emotion is a highly complex regulatory system in which each person faces an inner and an outer world, and at the same time shares something in the realm of relationships. This is obvious if you think of rage. At a recent conference on psychotherapy dealing with the topic of affect, one participant said, "It is quite clear. Rage means, 'You, out of my way!'" In my opinion, rage can also mean, "You, pay attention to me!" But in any case, it has the character of a signal from one person to another.

Affects and emotions do not enjoy a very good reputation— not only elated affects, but affects and emotions in general. Feelings elicit caution. The impression is that people get carried away. We have all learned that we should not let our emotions break out, and that if they do, or if we are neurotically impulsive, we should get ourselves under control.

Neurotically impulsive persons have the uncontrollable urge to destroy. After smashing everything up, they are desperately unhappy because they did not want to destroy anything. The existence of this neurotic form of emotional outbreak explains, in part, why emotions do not have a very good reputation.

Rationalistic and puritanical trends have also contributed to this suspicion and neglect. No problem arises as long as emotions are expressed in a moderate or sublimated form—for example, in beautiful writings full of feeling. "The danger inherent in euphoria," we hear, "is the tendency to go beyond all limits of decency. Transcending oneself is all well and good, but living beyond one's means is another matter."

As soon as feelings get a bit more archaic, we believe, trouble begins. Therapists are not exempt from this view. We are basically quite afraid of archaic affects, and every form of therapy permits affect only within a circumscribed range, as do the norms of everyday life. Here my first response is to note that emotions of depression have as much tendency to become immoderate as emotions of elation do. If you have ever seen how depression in a group multiplies geometrically, you know equally well what lack of moderation means. Just because it is excessively tragic instead of excessively comic does not make it more real or less dangerous. And affects can be very dangerous. Having one's consulting room smashed up is a disaster. Every now and then a therapist is murdered. I would not wish to minimize the impact of emotions; emotions literally mean something breaking into motion within us. The fact that they sometimes go overboard does not justify a policy of total neutralization though. Such a policy also results, as I have said, in the neutralization of involvement and caring. Everything then becomes apathetic and distanced. There is a great loss in the interpersonal realm, and the fear of closeness excludes all but walls between us.

When I began this book, I had great difficulty in deciding how to approach my topic because I did not want to focus exclusively on happy emotions. We do enough of that in everyday life, and it is false. I have spent more than ten years of my life telling people that grief is a positive emotion. I cannot suddenly think of positive emotions in a completely different sense.

Still, if you look at the literature [Ziegler, 1912; Nablowsky, 1884; Lersch, 1970; Schele, 1983], you soon get the feeling that ever since antiquity emphasis has been placed on the bestial and destructive side of the emotions: rage, aggression, anger, and depression. Their danger and their potential have been stressed to the neglect of the feelings of elation and fullness, which should have equal status as emotional realities.

I have come to the view that more attention should be given to all emotions, but especially the emotions of elation because a great deal is said about anxiety in depth psychology and in psychology as a whole; human nature itself is virtually derived from anxiety. We need only think of existentialist philosophy, in which the human being is filled with anxiety and yet finds the courage to be. Rage, too, is the subject of discussion now and then. Shame and guilt have received a good deal of attention, as have depression and grief. But joy, inspiration, hope, and related emotions are seldom spoken of, in spite of the fact that a major concern of every therapy—and every life—is the individual's search for happiness and high spirits. We want to be "in a good mood."

This is not to deny that by enduring anxiety we can emerge with a transformed emotional makeup, that desperation can reach its nadir and bounce back as hope. I want only to make the observation that psychology has fastened our attention on anxiety to such an extent that we are quite wary when it comes to surrendering ourselves to joy. (In poetry, matters are different. There are countless poems about joy, happiness, and contentment.)

Clearly anxiety is a fundamental emotion, but I do not believe that the essence of human nature can be defined solely on the basis of this one emotion. Moreover, anxiety often drives us into isolation, making us believe that we are solitary individuals, "loners flung into fate," as Heidegger said. If we are in a joyful mood, we are much more likely to connect with other people.

In existential philosophy, as well as in depth psychology, the nature of human beings has been described quite persuasively from the point of view of anxiety, with the accent on the solitariness of the individual or the community born of pure necessity. But as human beings, we have another possibility: to open up and connect with those around us. This may seem a bit threatening or naive. Opening up *sounds* good, but let's be realistic: We have to look out for ourselves. It is important to take note of these misgivings, because they shield us from our feelings of elation. A quite different description of human nature than the existentialist one is revealed by the emotions of joy and inspiration: a human nature based on solidarity, affiliation, and hope.

Under the influence of elated feelings, our sense of relatedness clearly changes. For example, arriving at a party, I may start looking at people critically, thinking, "I don't really want to have anything to do with this." Once the party is under way, though, I no longer behave this way, having forgotten about what made everyone so objectionable. What appeared too bourgeois now seems original; I no longer scrutinize and judge. A sense of relatedness prevails over criticism, which is of course exactly what the emotions of elation are accused of: They lift us out of the harshness of everyday reality, making us uncritical and blind to the depths of melancholia.

Joy implies solidarity, and solidarity implies generosity. Studies have been made in which children were shown films that they enjoyed very much [Izard, 1977]. Afterward, they each received fifty cents for watching the film, and a donation box was set up at the exit for the sake of children in poverty. The children who had enjoyed themselves gave substantially more money than the control children, who had seen a boring film and wanted to keep all their money for themselves. By the way, this example illustrates secondarily how emotions can be manipulated. By inspiring enthusiasm, it is possible to seduce people into doing things they do not really want to do. One need only think of mass hysteria. But this is no argument against an occasional surrender to elated feelings. Fear, anger, and shame can also be used to manipulate. Nothing in life is devoid of danger; only by ceasing to live can we avoid danger altogether.

The emotions of elation fill us and lift us up. The existentialist psychoanalyst Ludwig Binswanger [1955] described joy as "leaping and striding." We can imagine ourselves leaping for joy and in the process springing into the distance. But if we leap too high, we soon approach mania. Fear of mania is one of the main reasons the elated emotions are not valued very highly. Just as neurotic impulsiveness can go too far, the elated emotions can take us too far up, so that we risk plunging painfully back into reality.

Joy, inspiration, and hope take us into the distance; they exhilarate us, they stimulate us, and they promote both serenity and affiliation. It is more pleasant to be around people who are enthusiastic and cheerful than around those who are worried and gloomy. Nevertheless, enthusiastic persons are often labeled naive. Feelings of elation must be justified, and so must optimism in the wake of elated feelings. In fact, mistrust and skepticism toward elated feelings are sometimes carried to the extreme of saying, "Joy is nothing but a cover-up for anxiety, a reaction formation." In your delight, you are likely to be confronted with the question, "What are you repressing?" I think this is a fairly twisted attitude, and I suspect that a significant fear of joy is involved in it.

Of course, it is perfectly correct to observe that loud joy can be a cover for anxiety. I remember when I was young and cavorted with a group. We were actually quite afraid, but we assured each other that we were having a hell of a lot of fun. And by doing such a good job of assuring ourselves, we did actually experience something like joy. To others also it may have looked like joy, but I see now that it was a disguise for anxiety. This is still not to say that every joy is anxiety in disguise.

To describe joy, Binswanger gave us the elegant phrase "with each upward striving, a step into the distance." Someone who aspires to the heights obviously cannot be concerned with every pebble on the path. But such a person is accused of being frivolous, leaping over contradictions, letting things slide, being content to simply *be*, without asking any questions. In my opinion, as long as one's emotional repertoire does not consist of elated feelings alone, there may be nothing wrong with light-hearted behavior. I am not at all sure that talking out every conflict to its bitter end always brings a solution. Sometimes it is better to let a problem go for now, taking a running leap over it later. We burden ourselves enough with thinking; surely it is just as important to experience our emotions and just *be* once in a while.

If we have a pessimistic attitude, we have the feeling that we are in the way of things and that the world is pushing us around. In our pessimism we believe that this feeling does not need to be justified, for it is clear that things fall apart. By contrast, according to this attitude, our enjoyment needs to be justified: "What right do we have to be optimistic?" I simply cannot accept such an attitude. If the pessimists were right, the world would have gone under a long time ago, and yet it still lives. I do not pretend that it is in the best condition, but it lives. I fight against the view that the feeling of depression need not be justified whereas the feeling of joy or hope must be. How did it come to this?

Freud assigned the pleasure principle to the realm of the id. Here is one answer to the question of why we mistrust joy: Anything associated with pleasure has a negative overtone, since it is always infantile to a certain extent, implying irresponsibility. Playful and joyful enthusiasm is all very well and good—for children. A moment's reflection makes it clear that psychic maturity, according to this moral standard, approximates tragic renunciation, a resolve always to see the cloud and never the silver lining. In my view, psychic maturity also includes the ability to rejoice in becoming who we are—in the presence of a great deal of anxiety, depression, and anger, to be sure. I would be the last to deny these emotions their due; I simply stand for the equal rights of elation with dejection. I believe that psy-

chic maturity means more than tragic renunciation and acceptance of anxiety; it is also a matter of vitality, power, and happy
unfolding.

What do the writings of Jung have to tell us about joy?
Jung's theory of the archetypes offers a theoretical foundation
for the affects that accords well with other theories of affect.
His theory allows for a great variety of affects as well as for
fluid boundaries between them. And yet on closer inspection,
Jung's writings also reveal a certain prejudice in favor of a con-
frontation with anxiety and stress that tends to place the elated
feelings and moods in a category labeled "extraverted."

In *Psychological Types,* Jung differentiated extraverted and
introverted attitudes: Introversion is more inwardly oriented,
toward the psyche; extraversion is more outwardly oriented, toward the world. Careful study of Jung's theory of types does
not permit the categorical description of a person as either "introverted" or "extraverted." These are poles between which we
exist, sometimes closer to the extraverted side and sometimes
closer to the introverted side. Amateur psychology, however,
labels certain people as extraverts and others as introverts. Joy
and happiness, at times rather noisy, belong to extraversion according to this view. There is an implicit value judgment here.
Jung often emphasized that no judgment of value is implied in
the differentiation of attitudes. And yet over time, the quite
distinct view has arisen that introverts are the serious ones,
and that extraverts are the lightweights, the tender-minded.
We all know how easily tender-mindedness can become mind-
lessness. Thus the prejudice does exist that introversion is indeed more profound, and that extraversion should be regarded
with caution.

You will notice that I am advocating the emotions of joy
from various perspectives. I believe we should give these emotions more consideration. Might there even be ways of stimu-

lating them? It is conceivable that we would make more progress in therapy by stimulating a certain amount of joy than by
keeping our noses buried in the same problem that has still not
proved capable of resolution. We tend to believe that joy is a
gift, not something that can be deliberately created. To say,
"Come on, be glad," would be absurd, because joy cannot be
produced on command. In spite of our experience that joy is
something that happens to us, I persist in asking if there is no
way to stimulate and facilitate it.

Words of caution and reproach hinder us from serious consideration of what I hold to be a crucial psychological reality:
that happiness can also be a turning point. Therapy makes us
familiar with breakthroughs that occur when we have endured
our anxiety, when our desperation gives way to hope, which
is why we are often told, "Don't flee from your depressed feelings; go into them, for then something new can happen." Less
has been said about how happiness can also be a turning point.
Of course, it is essential to get anxiety under control and to
endure it; please do not think I have anything against working
with these emotions. I am for equal rights. Thus the elated emotions must also be seen as emotional turning points of potentially decisive significance for an individual's life.

Think of a time when you were very much in love. Think
about whether something new did not come into your life then.
At such moments we cast off the old Adam or the old Eve,
and what has been sleeping within suddenly awakens because
someone is there to tell you, yes, you are all of that; you are
wonderful and I love you. These are moments not only of the
greatest joy; they are also moments when real changes can take
place.

2.

Feelings, Affects, and Moods

I WOULD LIKE NOW to deal with a language problem. When I speak of the psychology of emotions, I include myself in the tradition of Jaspers, Bollnow, and von Uslar, according to which emotions, moods, feelings, and affects belong to a common genre. In the German psychological literature, emotion is often equated with affect, but in the American literature emotion always means feeling. It is extremely confusing.

Let us say that emotion is the inclusive term covering feeling, affect, and mood. Feelings can be perceived and named, are accompanied by images that we can communicate to others, and have definite causes and goals. Affects are more primary than feelings, shooting through us with an intensity that provokes a physical reaction and usually a social reaction, too. Mood has a less obvious cause; it describes the state and attunement of our being.

FEELINGS

By feelings I understand inherent tendencies or orientations toward experience (for example, love, hate, envy) at the moment when we become aware of them as specific phenomena to which we can assign a name or image. Feelings endure over a given time, transcending particular situations. "I have always been someone who easily got mad," or "I have always been impatient," or "I have always liked to have a good time." Particular feelings arise in particular areas of life and experience. You certainly know which feelings are typical for you in your professional world, or in the realm of love. It can be assumed that a limited number of feelings in a particular configuration characterize a given individual's personality.

Two qualities distinguish feelings from moods: Feelings can be named, and they demand something. When I invited you at the beginning of chapter one to reflect on what mood you were in, you may have noticed that you could say little more than that you were in a good mood, not in such a good mood, or simply "out of sorts." If you were able to give your emotional experience a definite name, it was probably a feeling. Maybe you experienced a bit of joy or anxiety. Maybe there was a feeling of interest. That would have been more than a mood; it would be a feeling that we could name. Such feelings are often connected with a fantasy. Jaspers [1965] calls these "root-like motions of the soul." I call them nameable feelings.

Feelings demand something of us or point very clearly to a situation of personal importance for us. If I get angry, it is because my anger wants something from me. My delight does not usually appear out of a clear blue sky; I am usually delighted about something—for instance, an effort that has been successfully completed or an unexpected turn of good fortune. One result of joy is to direct my attention to what has happened so that I am more readily moved to share my joy with others, to make joy for them and so forth. While moods are expressions of the way we are, feelings have an aim and are connected to cognition, hence to memory, thinking, and imagination. Feelings involve ideas, fantasies, and worldviews.

AFFECTS

I regard affects as complicated, intense, emotional events accompanied by clear physical reactions and bodily movements. Cognition is usually highly impaired by affect. In fact, a genuine affect renders us impervious to rational argument. Under the influence of affect, we contradict ourselves. Since our cognitive structures are all distorted, we do not see something the way it is; sometimes we do not see it at all. If we refer to Jungian psychology, we could speak of an affect as a complex that has been touched off.

In general, affect is the most primary emotional event, and feelings develop out of affects. Mood forms a background to both affects and feelings.

MOODS

To define mood we could use the expression "dominant tone of an experiential field." We could also speak of the atmospheric background that pervades and rules our experience. It is difficult to say what mood we are in, although we know that our moods play a decisive role in our experience. A mood is like background music: We live in it psychically even if we do not always notice it consciously.

It is extraordinarily difficult to pin down the mood we are in. It is easiest in the morning, when we get up and say, "Today I'm in a good mood" or, "Today I'm in a lousy mood." We look outside to see what the weather is like. Am I bright, foggy, or overcast? Mood may be a reflection of our environment. Mood can also be directly related to the dreams from which we have just emerged. We often notice that something in a dream has put us in a bad mood. Our moods are also related to the state of our bodies. Stomach pain may accompany a worse than usual mood. Mood is fascinating in the way it expresses both our physical and our psychic state, our relationship to the world and to other persons. A mood does not demand that we *do* anything, as feelings do. If I am angry, I want either to flee or to effect some change. But a mood is simply the way I feel at the moment, the state of my soul, a humor that pervades my being. Moser coined the term "state affect" to describe mood. I think "affect" is too strong to apply to mood, because we are dealing with a quiet encroachment upon the soul that precedes definite conceptualization.

We do not have many words for moods. We often compare moods with the weather. I am feeling bright and sunny, or cloudy and gray. Certain colors express moods: "I was in a black mood," or "I've got the blues." These are existential feelings. When we are in a really good mood, we say we are "glad to be alive."

The colors that we intuitively choose to wear say a great deal about our moods. "I just couldn't put that dress on today; I wasn't in the right mood." The dress did not fit the mood. Recently I was working with a woman going through a period of mourning. One day she came dressed in a beautiful, shining yellow dress. Until then, she had always come dressed in black. This stopped me short. She said, "You say that everyone in grief goes through these moments of joy. Today I just couldn't put on that black dress, so I put on a shining yellow one." A week later she came dressed in gray. A mood can be expressed in a color. It can also be expressed by painting a picture or by looking at daydreams. Somehow I must express my mood.

Someone who is very involved in music may say, "My mood is like a nocturne by Ravel." In German the word for mood, *Stimmung,* has to do with tuning. The word for one's basic temperament in German is *Gestimmtsein,* literally meaning attunement. The word for being in a bad mood, *verstimmt,* literally means being put out of tune. If I am in a bad mood, I will be out of tune; and if someone tries to strike a chord with me, it will sound sour. We warn others, "Don't spoil my mood," or, "Now I'm in a bad mood," in the knowledge that it is better not to talk to someone who is in a bad mood since that person is out of tune. We can be out of tune with ourselves, with our bodies, or with the outside world.

Each of us has a characterological mood that we recognize as our basic temperament, and when we stay within a certain range of that basic mood, we are considered even-tempered. We are very familiar with the ideal of being even-tempered, like a well-tempered piano (*Gleichgestimmtheit*). We know, though, that we can also experience mood swings, just as an instrument goes in and out of tune (*Stimmungsschwankung*). A clinical report in which it is written that a patient suffers from mood swings is not likely to be read as a report about someone who reacts very consciously to changes in his body, in the environment, in himself, or in his psyche. It will instead be read as a report about someone who is moody and not on an even keel, whose regulation mechanisms are not in good order.

We make an ideal of even temperament, but I would urge you to think about whether mood swings might not have an important function, too, at least within a certain range. A mood swing can be a reliable indicator that shows us when things are out of place or something is wrong (*stimmt nicht*). Of course if your mood changes all the time, so that one minute you are soaring up to heaven and the next minute you are down in the dumps, or you swing from aggressive to loving in quick succession, you will present difficulties for those around you. But I would like to turn the matter around for once by asking if these fluctuations of mood are not a sign that something has gone out of tune, that something in our lives must be changed to put us back in tune again. Might this very delicate signal notify us that something has gone wrong?

Moods clearly show the human being to be a "biopsychosocial unity" (von Uexküll and Wesiack, 1986). A biopsychosocial phenomenon implies the interrelatedness of body, psyche, and environment. This is especially clear in the case of emotional attunement. If you are able to watch your mood for a while, you will notice how many factors can disturb it: indisposition coming from the body, dreams coming from the psyche, or bad weather coming from the environment. It is much easier to be feeling fine inside when the weather is fair outside, unless you are in a deep depression. Things coming at us from every possible direction can put us out of tune, which actually means that we are no longer in harmony with ourselves. Moods make us very aware of the extent to which we partake of a biopsychosocial unity.

If you have the feeling that your basic mood has changed, this could be an indication that something crucial has happened in your life — or that something needs to happen. For example, it might indicate that you are not treating your body very well, or that an ever-present affect has finally gone away. It might also indicate that problems in your social environment need to be solved, or that new constellations in the psyche are demanding attention.

For instance, a man who had a serious depression that necessitated a temporary stay in a psychiatric hospital said, "I actually used to be a cheerful man. I was well liked, the life of the party. I made other people happy. And then suddenly I realized that I was always in such a nervous mood. I thought it must be because I was getting older." Others responded to his depression by telling him that he had finally become an adult. Here we arrive again at the theme of elated moods as something reserved for children; only children are allowed to enjoy themselves without inhibition. This man said, "I felt nervous. But I didn't change anything." He thought he was passing through a normal transition. He became seriously depressed. This may not have been necessary. He could have taken his radical change of mood as a signal that something basic in his life had gone wrong, and he could have attempted to discover what it was. Instead he interpreted the obscure change of his basic mood as a change for the better and was much too late in seeking help. People who experience this kind of basic mood change might want to think about when they began restricting their displays of joy. When someone who is basically cheerful becomes pensive — or quite depressed — he or she may experience the following sort of feedback: "I get the impression you are no longer unscathed by the seriousness of life."

A persisting change of basic mood can also be observed with physical diseases. Very often people who on the whole are reasonably calm and suddenly find themselves becoming anxious as their mood takes a downward plunge may find a physical explanation. For example, I was working with a woman in therapy who suddenly became very anxious, troubled, and depressed. I could not see anything coming from the inside or from the outside to explain this. So I sent her to a physician, who diagnosed a chronic infection of the kidney.

When we sense such radical changes of mood, we need to ask ourselves, What has actually happened in my life? These situations are often quite understandable. If you have lost someone important to you, your basic mood changes. Your basic mood should also change if you have a fulfilling experience. It just changes in a less obvious way.

But can we change a mood at will? Would it make any sense to do so? You certainly all know the situation of having work to do and not being "in the mood" to do it. What do you do? There are those who wait until they *are* in the mood.

This can take quite a while. There are those who say, "I can't worry about whether I am in the right mood or not," and do what they have to do. Among the latter group, some do get into the right mood; they just needed a push. But there are those whose mood only worsens. These people do not respond very well to the rigorous work ethic that says, "I don't care whether you are in the mood or not; go to it!"

Finally, there are people who have methods for putting themselves in the right mood. Some of them begin by doing something completely unrelated to the task at hand. For example, I have a colleague who reads Plato whenever he has to write a lecture, much to his wife's displeasure. He sits back in a chair in the living room and reads, while his wife says, "You have to write your lecture." He says, "I'm not in the mood." He reads Plato, and Plato puts him in the mood. Most of us have activities and favorite things that put us in the right mood. We have ways of "catching" a mood.

EXPERIMENT: EMOTIONAL HISTORY

I said above that certain basic, persistent feelings make up our personalities. (Researchers agree about this; see Izard or Bollnow, for example). These feelings can also become affects. I have written down a number of words that deal with emotions, and have organized them into clusters of related affects.

It is in the nature of emotions to evade clear description, which is why I have organized this incomplete and provisional list into clusters. Rage, for example, flows readily into anger or irritation; anger flows into guilt and then depression; irritation flows easily into anger, hate, or finally desperation. Joy goes together with satisfaction, cheerfulness, contentment, happiness, and love. My goal here is not to present a map of all emotions, but only a sample of some that are closely connected

29

Emotional clusters

rage — anger ⟨ hate
irritation
desperation

anxiety — fear — fright — shame

joy — mirth — happiness — love

expectation — longing — confidence — hope

expectation — disappointment — rage

anger — guilt — depression

joy — satisfaction — contentment — cheerfulness

distress ⟨ grief
anxiety

boredom — wonder — inspiration
contempt

jealousy — envy — hate — loneliness
— gloating

surprise ⟨ fright — anxiety
relief
gratitude

pity — generosity — compassion

patience — serenity — trust

joy — satisfaction — pride

hope — inspiration — joy

aversion — disgust — antipathy

to others in order to offer some key words to help us remember how our emotions have changed in the course of our life histories. I have in mind a complete model of emotions, which I will present in a future work.

As you study these emotional clusters, think about which of them best describe your present situation. Without thinking about it too long, choose four to eight clusters that are most characteristic of your life.

Now see if you can recall your first day at school. Picture yourself there. Try to remember which emotions were the most important then. Which emotions were the most intense? Are these the same emotions you chose as characteristic of your life? Of the emotions you have chosen, think about whether any of them are emotions of elation. Can it be that in your description of yourself, you have painted a picture of your ideal self, or a distorted and darkened picture of your real self? Do the emotions you think of as characteristic fit actual experiences and periods of your life?

The idea behind this experiment is that some emotions predominate throughout our entire lifetime or, to put it in terms of the theory of complexes, some basic themes in our lives present persistent difficulties while others change. You may have noticed that emotions from your childhood are not exactly the same as those which characterize your adult life. And perhaps you noticed that certain existential feelings have persisted.

I asked about whether your self-portrayal was idealized or distorted for a specific reason. Researchers on emotion hold the view that when people are asked to write down their emotions and then indicate the degree of each emotion that is characteristic of them, they are correct in their assessment by definition. But to those schooled in depth psychology, it is quite clear that people present idealized or distorted images of themselves. For this reason, I have found it important to ask persons who know me well, "Which emotions do you think are most characteristic of me?" Try this; then ask yourself if you are able to recognize the feelings reported to you, and if you have the impression that they have changed or not. Often they have.

In concluding this chapter, I would like to offer the example of a chain of emotions described by a forty-two-year-old man. He said that as a seven-year-old boy he was characterized by the following emotions: anxiety, longing, contempt, loneliness, and patience. As a twenty-one-year-old student he typically felt anger, hate, love, wonder, envy, and loneliness. You see how the loneliness remains, and how anxiety has been replaced by aggression, envy, and wonder. At the age of forty-two his emotional attunement was composed primarily of the feelings of loneliness, satisfaction, serenity, pride, and longing. The nervous seven-year-old child, who was so lonely that he could save himself only by means of arrogance, became aggressive at the age of twenty-one, when he was also filled with wonder for the world, in love, and consumed by envy of those who enjoyed greater successes. Envy produces loneliness. At the age of forty-two he had accepted that he was a lonely person, and this acceptance of himself afforded him calm and tranquility. Arrogance gave way to pride.

An emotional biography illustrates how certain emotions persist (loneliness, fear, probably also envy), and it reveals on the other hand unmistakable developments. We could go on to ask what events in this man's life led to the appearance of lively aggression and engagement with the world at the age of twenty-one and to the disappearance of these same emotions at the age of forty-two.

When we consider our biographies from the perspective of various emotions, we gain important access to the various basic temperaments that make up our nature at different stages of our lives, and this information allows us to recall the essential events that shape our life stories. We recall something other than what normally occurs to us when we tell of our lives; new pathways open up to our selves.

3.

The Interpersonal Context of Emotions

EMOTION IS AN INTENSELY PERSONAL PHENOMENON; it is an expression of the self. Yet emotion also has an interpersonal dimension, an interpersonal context. I want to consider three aspects of the interpersonal context of emotions. First, emotions are "caught" from others and "spread" to others in a kind of circular motion in our daily lives. Second, the self-image we have formed through our emotional histories predisposes us to some emotions more than others—linking us in a kind of larger circle with our own interpersonal past. Finally, the expression—verbal and nonverbal—we give our emotions as we interact with others both conditions our relations with them and affects the growth of our own emotional capacities.

CIRCLE OF EMOTIONS

Emotions, like moods, are very infectious. The "circle of emotions" is the best way I have found to describe what happens in emotional infection. If you walk through the streets smiling at everyone you see, your happiness will spread and many people will smile back, which makes you feel so friendly that you greet others with an even friendlier smile. If you walk through town feeling totally disgruntled, so that prickles seem to be growing on your back, you will soon realize that you trigger a different emotional reaction. You are giving a signal to others that says, "Don't get too close; I'm dangerous." They obey your signal and keep their distance. Maybe what you really wanted was just the opposite—someone to approach you rather than backing off. In any case, an emotional circle ensues. The emotion with which we greet others usually triggers that same emotion in them. Depending on the basic mood of this person, the effect of his or her emotion on us may be more or less long-lasting. But the momentary lightness of an otherwise depressed person will not leave us unaffected. This is one reason why so many people try to be friendly; then they at least ward off open hostility.

You are probably aware of how infectious a mood is. For instance, it is extremely difficult to live for any length of time with someone who is always sullen. The ongoing presence of a slightly aggressive person tends to put us in the same state, and it takes a real expert in dissociation not to be influenced by it. One of the problems we have in living together is that we cannot escape the moods of others. It is not so much specific actions or interactions that cause problems; it is the mood. We often hear people say, "It's not that he's done anything wrong; I just can't stand being around him."

Such a statement has to do with moods. But we are not conscious of this as long as we too are inside the mood, because inside a mood we are symbiotic, so to speak, with our inner world, with those around us, with the environment, with nature, and with our bodies. We must make a deliberate effort to separate ourselves. Nevertheless, this symbiosis is not just a negative thing. It is mood—and its symbiotic effect—that makes it possible for us to be very close to each other, which also means that we can take on the problems and moods of others.

EMOTIONAL HISTORY

In the last chapter, when we compared how we felt on our first day of school with how we feel now, we discovered that we have an emotional history. My emotional history is inseparably related to the emotional history of those around me. For example, if you were always led to understand that you were a cheerful child whom others were glad to see, you developed a happy self-image which gave you confidence that others took delight in seeing you. On the other hand, if you were told that you were a troublesome child, you adopted a self-image that put you in doubt about whether others were glad to see you, and you thought, "What must I do so that others are glad to see me?" A part of who we are comes from the mirroring we received and how we responded to it, especially during early childhood. Our emotional history affects our present lives in many ways—our emotions, our complexes, and our relationships.

EMOTIONAL EXPRESSION

We know about body language. We are aware of how our voices normally sound, and of how we sound when we get hysterical or start blaming, when we become suspiciously quiet or begin flattering. And we perceive the signals of others. We notice if people break out in sweat, if their faces go white or turn red, if their features get distorted. These signals are called gestures, gestures of expression, or expressive movements. On the basis of such gestures or expressive movements, we draw conclusions about the emotions behind them. We do this by means of empathy, as if asking ourselves, "How would I be feeling if I made this face? How am I feeling when I have this voice?" For example, when I realize that someone trying to speak is extremely frightened and is able to gather only enough air to let out a peep, I really suffer with him or her. This empathic resonance with other persons is one way to read their gestures.

Self-observation assures us that gestures often express true feelings. A gesture of fright may correspond to a real experience of fright, or a huge smile may indicate that you are really happy about something.

You can also check your own feelings against the perceptions of others. We normally receive nonverbal feedback indicating when we have been understood. If the feedback is appropriate to some feeling other than the one we are expressing verbally, it probably indicates we are giving off nonverbal signs (gestures) that we feel something different.

The importance of these expressive movements is apparent from their absence when you talk on the telephone. Quarrels on the telephone, for instance, should be avoided for the following reason: When you confront someone, you look each other in the face, and you push yourself to the critical limit, close to the point where the other person gets angry and leaves — that is, to the point where contact is broken. As long as you see the person, his or her entire body, you can usually stay at the critical limit without breaking contact. But there are always surprises, and if you cannot see the other person, as on the telephone, the danger is much greater that one of you will lose your composure. Moreover, it is much worse to have contact broken on the telephone than in your presence, where you still have a chance to try out the arts of seduction known to you. This demonstrates the importance of gestures.

The interpretation of dreams cannot take place on the telephone either, except with someone you know extremely well. Here in America, even analysis is carried out on the telephone. For me that would be absolutely impossible, simply because I work with emotions, often at the critical limit. I need the information gestures give about those emotions.

But the question remains whether we read emotionally expressive gestures correctly. We assume that we know what these expressions mean. And yet it has been demonstrated that anxiety, for example, triggers glandular secretions and facial contortions that are virtually indistinguishable from those triggered by rage. A therapist may say, "I sense anxiety," and you answer, "No, I feel rage." I often have the impression that the name we give to a feeling is primarily a matter of education. In a family where everyone is anxious, a great deal will go by the name of anxiety; in a family where everyone is angry, a great deal will go by the name of anger. The matter is made even more complicated by the fact that emotional gestures can be falsified and deliberately performed as well. For example, if I am in a conversation and I notice that my conversation partner will be dissatisfied if I do not become indignant about the issue we are discussing, I face a choice: either I make a performance of what I don't really feel, or else I offend my partner and prepare for a talk about why I was not indignant. Self-observation reveals that we periodically perform gestures without any emotion behind them.

Are you a good actor or actress? The really good ones can think themselves into a feeling to the point of intense identification with it. When an actor laughs or cries, this may in fact be genuine feeling and not only an empty gesture. But it further confuses our ability to interpret gestures.

An emotion becomes genuinely one's own when gestures correspond to feelings. This correspondence is not so simple to test. Empathy alone is not enough; conventions of emotional performance must also be taken into account. When you are in a country with a culture that is foreign to you, for example, you notice how difficult it is to read the emotions of others simply by trying to put yourself in their shoes. You have to know something about the rules of the game—the norms—as well. In Swiss culture, stiff, formal laughter is a norm at certain parties. The absence of such laughter at these parties may indicate the presence of a genuine emotion. If I am an outsider and I really feel like laughing, how should I express this feeling? Unfamiliar with the game rules, I am unsure about whether I can surrender to the emotion. Someone trying to understand my emotional situation would be hopelessly confused if calling on empathy alone; she or he would also have to consider how the scene is being performed.

Another problem in interpreting gestures is that we are often so cut off from our emotions that we can bring to expression little more than empty gestures. Out of touch with our feelings, we substitute conventional gestures.

Though I am saying that emotions are expressions of the self, it is well known that we often display the expressions of an emotion when we are not actually moved by the emotion itself. Then we are not authentic. Emotional sincerity means basing our gestures on real feelings. This involves a certain social risk, since some feelings are not well tolerated, or are tolerated only within certain limits. If we decide we no longer want to hide behind empty shells, then we will have to allow certain emotions more room. We will have to let ourselves laugh louder, cry louder, and shout for joy. If we wish to come into contact with feelings of elation, we must cast aside our masks, divest ourselves of our routine smiles, wrinkled noses, and disapproving glances, and free ourselves for real emotional expression.

PART II

Joy

4.

Joy as Elevation

IN INGEBORG BACHMANN'S NOVEL *Malina,* two male characters, Ivan and Malina, compete for the narrator's attention. Ivan wants to seduce the narrator into life, Malina into death. Ivan, commenting on notes that the narrator has made for books that deal with death and other somber themes, says, "Why always such books? There must be other books that, like EXULTATE JUBILATE, make you jump out of your skin for joy. You do jump out of your skin for joy, don't you? So why don't you write that way? Bringing more of this misery to the marketplace, multiplying it in the world is a wretched business. Such books are all offensive." This statement moves the narrator to write a single, glimmering passage—designed to make you jump out of your skin for joy—in an otherwise somber book. I ask you to imagine the text in vivid pictures, because emotions and pictures are very closely related.

> A shower of words is born in my head and then a lamp is lit. A few syllables flicker up. Bright commas fly out of all the sentence boxes, and periods that were once black inflate themselves and float like balloons to the ceiling of my mind, because in that book, that marvelous book that I am beginning to find, everything will be like EXULTATE JUBILATE [exulting and rejoicing]. If there really were such a book, and one day there must be such a book, you will throw

yourself on the floor for joy just from reading one page. You jump for joy; it does you good; you read more and bite your hand to keep yourself from screaming out loud for joy. You can't stand it, and when you sit on the window sill and read more, you throw confetti down on to the people walking in the street so that they stand there, amazed, as if they had stepped into a carnival. You throw down apples and nuts, dates and figs, as if it were St. Nicholas' Day. You lean out of the window without fear of heights and scream, "Listen, just listen. Look, just look. I have read something wonderful. Do you mind if I read it to you? Come closer everyone; it is too wonderful." And they begin to stand still and pay attention. More and more people gather together, and Mr. Breitner offers a greeting for a change. He no longer has to use his crutches to prove that he is the only cripple. "How do you do?" he croaks in a friendly voice. "Good day." And the fat opera singer, who only dares to go out of her house at night, always coming and going in taxis, gets a bit thinner. In a single moment she loses a hundred pounds. She shows herself in the stairwell, theatrically striding, without shortness of breath, to the mezzanine where she begins to sing coloratura with a voice twenty years younger, "Cari amici, teneri compagni!" And no one says condescendingly, "We have heard better from Schwarzkopf and from Callas." Even the epithet "silly old goose" has vanished from the stairwell. And the people on the third floor have been rehabilitated. An intrigue has fizzled out. The joy lingers so powerfully because there is finally such a marvelous book in the world. And I go to find the first page for Ivan. I make a mysterious face because I want it to be a surprise.

The book that should have been, was never actually written. The novel *Malina* is one part of a trilogy called *Ways of Death,* and at the end of *Malina* the first-person narrator vanishes into a wall and says, "It was murder." Not a happy ending. Yet this one passage says a lot about joy.

Many different aspects of joy are portrayed here in such a way that the archetypal configurations behind them show through. The idea is that joy can be infectious even in imagination. It is not absolutely necessary to have a direct experience of joy; the prospect of a really delightful book is enough to fill us with joy. This prospect must be celebrated — this EXULTATE JUBILATE that has been set to music so many times. Then come the words belonging to joy: A lantern is lit, syllables shimmer, everything floats upward. These are symbols for expressions of joy. You may be aware that when you laugh, the corners of your mouth normally curve upward; your face floats a little. Your eyes start to glow. Flickering and glowing are facial expressions. You leap for joy, or at least you would like to. The effect of joy is to counteract the pull of gravity and thus represents the force of levity. No wonder we always hear that joy is playful. With joy we overcome resistances and so naturally find a way to transcend ourselves.

The expression "to jump out of your skin for joy" sums up the entire matter. When we view this expression symbolically, we notice the motif of sloughing off the skin. This would mean that we could receive a new skin, which would be a major transformation, as symbolized by the healing power of the serpent. In psychotherapy, it has become a matter of convention that tolerance of depression and anxiety makes great changes possible. I have no doubt about this, and yet I think that experiences of happiness can change us no less, as suggested by the saying, "to jump out of one's skin for joy."

Now to continue with the Bachmann text, "She bites her hand to keep from screaming out loud for joy." We seldom give free reign to joy, which we feel would be childish. We are too grown-up to abandon ourselves to joy. We must control ourselves, biting our hands if need be in order to keep from screaming out loud.

After biting her hand, the narrator sits down on the window sill because she can hardly stand it. Joy tolerates no isolation. Joy is the emotion that lets down our guard, for better or worse. Joy opens us up; she opens the window and looks down at the people in the streets. Joy calls for merry display; Bachmann's narrator throws confetti. This reminds me of the Swiss Fasnacht carnival at the beginning of Lent when we try to be joyful. Sometimes it is only an empty shell of joy; it is not easy for everyone at the same time to get into a festive mood. But confetti expresses much more. When we are delighted, life is bright and colorful, in contrast to the dullness and gray of depression. Color expresses life.

In addition, when we are joyful, we can open up and give something away; we can throw it into the streets. The narrator shares not only confetti but also sentences with the people in the street. Opening up, giving words, giving the gift of a book to the world, throwing confetti.

The result is the cessation of gravity; the emotion of joy suspends gravity. The cripple suddenly offers his greetings, emphasizing the connection of people with each other. He no longer has to feel isolated and different because he is a cripple; instead, he belongs. Gravity literally disappears for the opera singer; losing one hundred pounds in a single moment is not bad. Her role is also introduced because singing is a way of expressing joy, something we are likely to do when we are feeling happy.

I have asked many people how they express their joy, and some very interesting things come to light. "I just walk faster," or "I take three and four stairs at a time, and I usually trip and fall in the process," or "I sing loud and out of tune," or "I sing loud and beautifully," or "I whistle because singing attracts too much attention." Look and see what you do when you feel joy. Joy's lightness lends itself to the making of sounds; its element is breath, spirit, and sky.

As Bachmann writes, joy has to do with beaming, shining, and glowing. One of the expressive gestures of joy is the beaming of the eyes, but not only the eyes; in true delight, the entire body beams. I realize it is not customary to speak of the body as beaming, but I can think of no better way to describe what happens. In any case, it is my opinion that the entire body can beam. The movements that accompany joy are always ascending movements. Bachmann writes of rising balloons, an image that suggests that joy suspends gravity.

Joy moves us upward and outward, toward ecstasy, toward others. It opens us, leads us to give things away, bonds us with others, suspends gravity, inspires us to sing and to make friends. The song that says, "Dear friends, tender companions," suggests a love that is connected rather than explosive. Joy and love can, of course, complement and intensify each other. A certain amount of joy is an essential ingredient in every collaboration. When joy is present, affiliation takes the place of backbiting, and paranoia disappears. The need to say bad things about those who think differently subsides. Intrigues come to a halt.

Moreover, although joy moves us upward and outward, it also has the inward aspect of helping us to experience ourselves. It is true to the nature of joy that Bachmann would describe not herself so much as what she does. Joy is the state in which we are least likely to reflect on ourselves. In the moment of delight, we *are;* there is nothing we have to *do.*

The passage also clearly expresses a secure sense of self when the narrator sits on the window sill free of dizziness. You should know that in Bachmann's next novel, *Der Fall Franza* (*The Case of Franza*), the main character suffers constantly from a fear of heights. The absence of dizziness in the present text points to a momentary state of health and well-being.

Joy promotes trust in oneself; when we are joyful, we feel self-confident and accept ourselves, knowing that our existence is not a matter of indifference. To put it the other way around, when we accept ourselves, we are likely to be delighted in and to feel accepted by the world, experiencing an affinity with that which transcends us, with other persons, and with the spiritual. This is the basis for solid self-esteem. The moment we accept ourselves, our inner being, and the world around us, we dwell in joy. We accept what is, and at the same time we welcome what is to be. Whenever we are considering how we might stabilize our fluctuating self-esteem, we are presented with a spectrum of possibilities: making conscious previously repressed complexes, interpreting dreams, exercising physically, seeking out friends. There is nothing to be said against any of these possibilities. But the highly sought-after feeling of being one with oneself, of being whole, is also contained in the moment of joy, along with a sense of vitality and maybe even of freedom.

Joy is very much related to fantasy. Ingeborg Bachmann referred to fantasy, and I asked you to fantasize. When we are joyful we are more imaginative, and possess a greater storehouse of ideas. However, they are not always the best ones. Like joy, fantasy has a lifting effect without any particular goal, for fixation on a goal prevents delight. In fantasy, we are wholly present to ourselves on the one hand, and far beyond ourselves on the other.

Its intimation of a fellowship with that which transcends us is probably the most characteristic feature of joy. Joy helps us to experience that fellowship and allows us to lose ourselves in it. Joy is inclined toward transcendence, transcendence of present relationships and of the world's resistance. Every movement connected with joy, even a quiet joy, is an elevating movement, relieving us of our normal weightiness, causing us to rise up and see matters from another perspective. This elevation is not without anxiety; if we rise too high, we exceed the limits of gravity altogether. Bachmann can write of balloons that stop at the ceiling of the mind; but if we were to become balloons ourselves, we might float out beyond any such restraints into the absolute.

The feeling of self-esteem that we experience with joy is natural self-acceptance. It may be the best self-esteem of all; for a moment we are sure of ourselves without question. The highest expression of delight is this self-acceptance. If self-acceptance is too enthusiastic, it can become problematic. But with the natural self-acceptance of joy, one *feels* important without having to *be* important, since it goes without saying that one *is* important. Natural importance and self-acceptance that requires no demonstration lead to openness.

Here again is the dimension of transcendence that relaxes rigid observance of ego boundaries. In joy, we are not distrustful; we are naive. Not expecting evil, we do not close ourselves off; we let down our guard. Thus we can be seriously injured if something evil comes to us after all. Many people protect themselves from being hurt by denying themselves too much joy. This protection is very costly. Natural self-acceptance that need not be insisted on and openness act together to give the self a feeling of vitality, as well as a certain kind of superiority, not of power but of transcendence. Rising above life's resistance, we attain a perspective from which our problems are easier to solve. The experience of joy can produce a noticeably balanced self-esteem. Something that usually requires massive compensation and a barrage of grandiose ideas can be reached simply through joy. But we do not always take conscious note of occurrences of joy. Sometimes we are delighted without even noticing, without thinking of it as anything special. I think it is so important to perceive the moment of joy. On the basis of the self-esteem and openness given by joy, we can relate to others with the feeling that we want to share, to cultivate friendships, and to be related in general. Communal life takes on color. Hearing all these testimonies of joy, not only from Ingeborg Bachmann but from all sorts of people, I can only say, "Be glad, so that all these wonderful things can come to fruition." Obviously, it is not so simple.

5.

Sources of Joy

I HAVE ASKED MANY PERSONS what delights them and gives them joy. The first source of joy that occurred to many was delight in themselves. Delight in themselves was similar to pride in themselves, arising naturally in connection with abilities, with beauty, and usually also with work that was well done or came out better than expected. For example, a respondent might say, "I can play the piano so beautifully," or "When I am creative, I feel great and I am delighted with myself." An apology invariably followed, with such statements as, "One shouldn't really say that, but you asked." We have difficulty in simply admitting delight with ourselves for having done a good job.

We all know that without this joy a great deal of work would never get done, for it is often this joy that motivates us to keep on working. For example, if someone has written a rather poor essay, and yet you can convince him or her that many things turned out very well in it, with only certain things not turning out so well, then he is not robbed of his joy, and there is still a good chance he will supply what is missing. Yes, the motivation of joy can persuade us human beings to work. Why would so many people make the huge effort involved in mountain climbing if it were not for this joy that keeps motivating them, giving them the vitality to press on toward greater joy? Delight in oneself is not generally the subject of polite conversation. But in a survey that I conducted at the University of Zurich, students anonymously listed delight in themselves — their physical appearance, intellectual competence, and whatever else they liked about themselves — as grounds for joy.

The second most frequently given source of joy among those I have asked is delight in the joy of others. Here a circle of joy is begun that we are most familiar with in the case of love. If you suddenly show a great deal of joy in someone, that person will often respond with joy. This sets a circle of joy in motion by which we affirm each other and share much fantasy. When mutual delight ends, imagination slacks off, mutual affirmation ceases, and major problems develop. Mutual delight is very important, but it can sometimes delude people into believing that they are in love, when actually they are simply feeling delight in the joy that has been created.

The third most frequently named source of joy is the opportunity to give joy to others. This has to do with a lifting of ego boundaries, a relaxation of defenses, permission to be and to reveal oneself, an opening of the self that is best expressed in the giving of a gift. Here the fear may arise that we are giving away too much of ourselves. It may be another symptom of our pathological way of dealing with joy that we are usually careful not to open up too much. When we are overjoyed, we sometimes give away secrets that in retrospect we wish we had kept. Joy's way of opening us up and of relaxing our habitual ego boundaries is very important.

Related to this opening of ourselves is our pleasant surprise when something unexpected breaks into life, when something new occurs that we never dreamed of. Then joy, expectation, and hope — emotions associated with a sense of discovery — are awakened. Discovery is a source of great pleasure for most of us.

There is often a feeling in joy that something has come to us that we did not really earn, since we did not work for it in a disciplined fashion. This is similar to what in religion is called grace. It is the joyful character of being, a deviation from the rule that we always have to work for everything. Some things come as a simple twist of fate. Many absolutely irksome things are decreed by fate, but we should not overlook the pleasant surprises that life also has to offer. Receiving something that is not actually ours is a source of joy that makes us cautious, however, for we are never completely sure if we are really entitled to what we have received and have taken such delight in. Many people hide their joy for fear of the envy of the gods. I am much more afraid of the envy of human beings.

Dreams as well as fantasies can trigger joy. I have attempted to collect dreams of joy from many persons, and their reaction is stereotypical: "I can never write it out so beautifully as I dreamed it," they say. "I prefer to leave it alone." That is a shame. We human beings seem to have difficulty with language, difficulty in giving adequate expression to situations that have stimulated joy, that is, expression that does not reduce the emotion of joy. Thus we keep these dreams to ourselves, often without even writing them down. This also means that we neglect the oases of joy that issue from our dreams, dreams which let us know that life is going well. Can you recall dreams that have resulted in joy? If we are searching for joy in our lives, then we are also concerned with the rediscovery and reevaluation of dreams and fantasies that contain joy.

Joy is triggered when something familiar appears instead of something foreign we have been anxiously expecting. For example, as a Swiss citizen I am traveling in Japan and suddenly run into another Swiss citizen.

Joy accompanies the disappearance of anxiety and pain. If you have been under stress, if something unpleasant has been agitating you, you will experience joy—if not a loud joy—when such pressures go away. We see this clearly in the treatment of persons in mourning. They reach the point when they have the feeling, "But now I can live again; the depression is going away," and they rediscover their huge delight in trees, in life, and in other persons. The initial joy fades again later, but the phenomenon of a rediscovered capacity for joy when pain and anxiety disappear is worthy of serious consideration. And yet I mention it only at the conclusion of my survey of the different sources of joy for two reasons. First, in spite of the fact that it is often held to be one of the most common sources of joy, in my survey it was only occasionally mentioned. Second, I want to look at joy from a different perspective. Rather than seeing joy as our reward for having endured anxiety or pain, I would like to show that joy is constitutive in our lives, not derived, something that can even coexist with pain and anxiety. If you think of times of war, you get the impression that in the face of disaster and cruelty a talent arises for enjoying the moment and for taking delight even in the most dire circumstances. Enjoying yourself has a great deal to do with being able to delight in today without asking what will happen tomorrow or expecting that things will only continue to be bad.

Collective creativity is a source of joy: something growing within a group that emerges as a new entity. Nature, beauty, and the process of becoming inspire joy. Culture is a source of joy. Joy derives from whatever one finds good or harmonious. We feel joy when body, psyche, and the world around us are in tune, when we can affirm existence, especially under the aspect of increase and intensification of being. We are joyful when something grows, when we have the feeling that new areas of life are becoming available to us, when we become freer and more daring. We experience these situations as an intensification of being, but also as a surprising gift. The same joy can grip us when persons we are connected with or close to open new vistas and cover new ground on their path through life. There are lots of occasions for joy, but we can think of joy as a way of feeling, of being that underlies our particular responses and which we tap into when the occasion offers itself. I think it is important not only to recognize when we are in a joyful mood, but also to perceive that we are beings of joy. We can do this when we take continual notice of situations that stimulate joy, when we search for them as far as we are able. We experience ourselves most clearly as joyful beings when we reconstruct our biographies of joy.

6.

Biographical Reconstructions of Joy

RESEARCH ON THE EMOTIONS and therapeutic work with emotions must be biographically oriented because our feelings have a history. Thus our joy has a history as well, which we can examine by asking such questions as, What in my life has given me joy? How have I expressed my joy? How does joy affect my experience of myself? How does it affect my relationships? How do I keep control of joy? What spoils it? These are question that we can consider throughout our lives. Or we can reflect on how the joy that we experience now has changed from the joy that we experienced as small children. This can be done very systematically, by reconstructing a biography of joy. I encourage you to write one for yourself.

I call it biography rather than case history because case history suggests disease, and for the moment I would like to bracket the investigation of pathology. It is fascinating to reconstruct your own biography. Replacing case history with biography, then, I would like to look at what we have become from the perspective of various aspects of joy.

It is a current fashion to reconstruct our biographies from various perspectives, an approach that offers us the opportunity to see our lives suddenly in new ways. By the time we are mature adults, we will probably have told our biographies countless times anyway, and in countless ways. Many people have a "narrative" biography that may be more or less fictional, depending on how playful or how revealing they wish to be. They may emphasize different strands in their biographies for different listeners. Or new insights or emphases may cause them to tell their biographies differently.

Shifting perspectives can reveal radically new dimensions of our lives. It is strange how milestones and transitions that never seemed worthy of notice can suddenly take on another, brighter light. Reconstructing a biography of joy removes us from our usual biographical treadmills and habitual conceptualizations. Once again we discover a new story about ourselves; perhaps we even creatively construct one.

The investigation can be carried out with varying degrees of intensity. Usually we proceed chronologically, by asking what we can recall at successive ages. I agree with taking this chronological approach, guided by a specific set of questions: How have I become what I am? What were the important aspects of this process? What has the nature of joy been in my life? In what situations was I really happy? How did I feel? How did I express my joy?

There is one more important question to ask: What has become of my joy? The point of a biography of joy is not only to locate situations from my past with which I can identify, for example, as a joyful child, but also to discover the fate of my joy. Or, having gathered together various past situations, I can identify with the entire development of joy that has taken place in my life. The materials that we use for our reconstructions are memories in the first place, and stories in the second. Much of what we think of as memory is actually derived from the stories we have heard others tell—stories told by parents, siblings, playmates, and friends; stories told by photos, diaries, and old toys. If you grew up in a house where your old toys have been saved, find some opportunity to go back to see them and evoke the memories residing within them.

In reconstructing your biography of joy you can also use drawings, and dreams of childhood joy. Try to recall a movement that you made as a child which brought you great joy. In one section of your reconstructed biography of joy, write down what you yourself remember. In another section, for the sake of comparison, write down what others remember about you. But do not give this comparison inordinate weight.

A few other suggestions: Recall what you were told about joy as a small child. Were you told anything at all? Now try to recall an early memory of joy from your childhood. Can you think of a situation in which you were very happy? It is best if you think of joy as an affect. Let an image come to you of yourself as a child who felt great joy. This may help you to discover how joy was aroused in you and how you expressed it. Ask yourself if other people were around. What effect did joy have on your relationships? Or was there no one else around? Did you share your joy with others, or did you keep it to yourself? Then ask yourself if the answer to this question helps explain why you either share your joy as an adult, or keep it to yourself. Do you find it more pleasurable to feel joy when others are there to share it with you? Or do you prefer to be glad in secret? As a child, how did your joy fade away? These are some suggestions for further investigation, which can of course be carried out with respect to your entire past. Or you could simply ask the question, Which times in my life were filled with great joy?

The reconstruction of a biography of joy has essentially two goals. One is to identify with ourselves as joyful children, recollecting ourselves and seeing what we did with this joy. The other is to establish a relationship with our present lives by ask-

ing such questions as, How does what I have remembered function today? Does it explain why I always share my delight or
keep it to myself?

The following example is an excerpt from a biography of
joy by a thirty-six-year-old woman, married, and the mother
of four children, who suffered on several occasions from depres-
sions with fairly serious suicidal tendencies and was hospital-
ized more than once. Her biography of joy was written down
after two years of therapy, at which time she was feeling much
better. I am deliberately choosing a biography of joy by someone who was depressed — someone who did not find it so easy
to go "up," being bound to the weight and resistance of the
world. The impulse for a biographical reconstruction came from
her when she discovered that I was giving lectures on the topic
of joy.

"It is strange that you should talk about joy," she told me.
"I could never do that. I am doing very well now, but I realize
that I am someone with little joy in life. I have always been
a joyless person; I come from a joyless family, and I believe my
present family is also joyless. What is this all about?" This was
her impetus for pursuing the theme of joy. I do not think she
was completely correct in saying that she was totally lacking
in joy, but there was something to her claim. I, too, had the
impression that she was a woman quite removed from joy, for
whom low spirits were more readily expressed than high spirits.

I asked her how others had described her as a baby with
respect to joy. "They told me that as a child I was full of joy,
she discovered. She was the third child. "They told me I practically fell out of the cradle whenever anyone came near me."
She seems to have expressed her joy with her entire body, the
way babies do at a certain age. They beam with their entire
bodies. "All babies do that," she said. "Mine also did it at a
certain age." When I asked her about their individual differ-

ences, she conceded that there are children who express more joy and children who express less.

Then she spoke for some time about her own children, the feelings they expressed, and her own feelings. And here joy became conscious again. "When the children would greet me so overjoyed, I too beamed with joy. Then of course the children were even happier to see me, shouting and cheering." This may be one way joy is produced in children: by sharing joy with them. The child's joy intensifies the mother's joy, which in turn intensifies that of the child.

Then I asked her what the first joy was that she could remember. She thought of the time she had received a rocking horse for Christmas. She was four and a half. She could piece the memory together quite well. She recalled photographs of herself on the rocking horse. She had held on tight to a huge mane of genuine horsehair and looked proudly about herself as if to say, "What do you want? I'm on this horse. There's no more to be said." She remembered how important the horsehair had been to her. She could feel her way back into the situation. "There was a lot of joy," she said, "and a lot of pride. I had the whole horse all to myself." She chased away her siblings by shrieking. This expressed a feeling of delight in herself and in the world; all was well with the world. You can see here the harmony of psyche, body, environment, and at the same time the reception of something new that may not have been earned.

Then I asked her how she expressed her joy. By shrieking at her sisters to fend them off, she first responded, adding that she also expressed it by refusing to get down from the horse; apparently she fell asleep there after singing for some time. Then she recalled that singing was always her way of expressing joy— loud singing.

Once we have gone back in our memories to a time of joy

that was very meaningful so that we can really feel the joy again, other memories follow in rapid succession. The most difficult part is getting started. We can certainly identify with this little girl and feel her joy. Once our emotions come into play, the identification occurs spontaneously.

The woman's next memory was of a time when she was a bit older. "I was helping my grandmother," she recalled. "I did that a lot. She praised me. I was full of pride and joy. I helped her even more, became even sweeter in her eyes; we exchanged a lot of hugs and kisses. I remember how much she loved that. She was delighted, which pleased me even more, and so I tried to do more to delight her. I became busier and busier with joy." She took quite some time to let that sink in. I have heard such situations from various people, and I am familiar with them personally. Then she said, "I was practically head over heels with joy."

I asked her, "How did this scene end?" I was thinking about how such scenes often end with something going wrong. When joy accumulates so intensely and the circle of joy reaches the point of ecstasy, it often ends abruptly—for instance, by someone falling down and hitting her head. She said she did not know how it ended, but then continued thinking. "With my own children, this is something I really do not like," she said. "At a certain point, they get so overexcited. The whole situation gets so overexcited." I asked her what she does at this point. "I tell them to go and clean up their rooms." She was surprised by her own reaction, which gave our conversation a completely different tone. We understood this as the termination of joy: When surrounded by three or four overstimulated children, the situation became a matter of survival for her. Her other method of coping was to leave. Then she tried to recall how her grandmother had dealt with the situation. "Grandma just disappeared, and then I did something else."

Now she became very interested in this being "head over heels" with joy, in the circle of joy, for she had seen the connection to her present life. "I kept doing that for a long time," she continued. "Whenever someone gave me something to enjoy, I tried to give them something to enjoy in return. And the more joy I was able to give, the more I tried to give even more." I think this is a very human way of behaving, which we could call the maximization of joy: repeated attempts to increase joy until joy reaches its limit.

A circle of joy can produce a certain narcissistic susceptibility. Some people are incapable of refusing any request if you say something nice to them, such as "I am glad to see you," or anything that implies an expression of joy. If someone says something nice to you, you really have to be nice if you want to keep the odds in your favor that they will express even more joy in seeing you. Thus you sometimes promise things that you do not actually want to do, in order to obtain the self-acceptance and self-esteem that come from experiencing joy. Suddenly you find yourself entangled in unwanted obligations brought on by your anticipated joy. This woman, with her depressive constitution, had to put up a massive fight against her narcissistic susceptibility, as she had long been in the habit of falling into its trap. If someone showed delight in her, without even waiting to see what would be asked of her, she would automatically ask, "Can I do something for you?"

Narcissistic circles of joy have become internalized by many persons and are applied quite calculatingly, for instance, when someone deliberately pays a compliment in order to follow it up later with a demand. Parents do this, as we all do with each other now and then. It is a shame that we cannot learn that it takes nothing more than joy to reproduce joy. It seems that joy is so often employed for manipulative ends.

This woman then talked about how she fought her narcissistic susceptibility. There was another memory from school, when she was perhaps eight years old. She didn't like school; she would rather have played. Then she remembered how much she enjoyed playing. She spoke of how much pleasure she had had in playing with abandon. It was a quiet joy which gave her contentment. She did not enjoy school, where she passed the time thinking about what she would do when she was back at home again, playing. I asked her what she played. "Family," she replied. While at school, she would plan and look forward to who would be the child today, what would be cooked, who the husband would be, and who the lover would be. The lover was an important part of the game because her father had one. Now talking with ease, she returned to her experiences at school. She was especially good at singing. Most of all, she liked merry songs, especially when shouting them out loud. That was fantastic: screaming rather than correct singing, a little bit off-pitch, loud and off-pitch. Singing is an expression of joy for many of us, and there are perhaps more of us who would rather shout than sing correctly, because shouting is more vital.

"Then life became less joyful," she continued. "We had to pay attention in school. We had a teacher who made us sing nicely." I asked her how that came about. "That came with the move. We moved into a more urban area. Father got a new job. I recall that now. We had a new teacher who made us sing nicely. And grandmother was gone. Strange, I never thought of that." Her mother became depressive shortly afterward, and spent more than six months in a hospital. Her older sister doggedly took over management of the household. "There was nothing more to laugh about," she said. This passage, not present in her case history, makes quite an impression in her biography of joy, striking us with her sudden inability to enjoy anything. In her case history, this part of her life was described as follows: "We then moved into an interesting part of town. I had new friends. My mother soon became sick and had to go to the hospital."

We see here how the perspective provided by the biography of joy systematically reveals situations in which all joy has disappeared and allows us much easier access to the emotions associated with these memories. When we consider all that happened to her and the aspects of her life that underwent change, we recognize that this must have been a time of great stress for this little girl. There was the move, the loss of her grandmother with whom she had experienced great joy, the loss of an existential feeling that had expressed itself in loud singing, the loss of her mother for a significant period of time, and thus the loss of her childhood.

In terms of "life-event research" [Datan and Ginsberg, 1975], she experienced five or six "stress factors," which would have given her every reason to contract an illness. She did not get sick, but she did say as an adult, "Life became emptied of joy." This was an important realization for her, because she had been under the impression that being a joyless person was due to a lack of effort and that more joyful persons were those who had more time to pursue joy. Here she became conscious that too much had broken into her life for joy to be manifest at that time.

Then I asked her about quiet joys. Most people have quiet joys during times they describe as joyless. In your reconstructed biography of joy, I want to urge you to take these quiet joys quite seriously. If you have the impression that there was a time that was totally devoid of joy, think about whether a quiet, discreet joy might not have been present nonetheless. Such joys are not to be revealed to just anyone, but since you do not need to show your biography of joy to just anyone, you should feel quite free to write them down.

When I asked this woman about her quiet joys, at first

nothing occurred to her, but then she recalled baby-sitting for a young couple nearby who had laughed a lot. Then she realized that this time spent with babies had been very important to her. She herself had had four children.

Here she required another push, so I asked her about her first love. First love is another moment filled with joy. She thought it over and then described him to me. She could still see him quite vividly. "I *did* like doing things with him. I *did* take delight in him. And I found it quite beautiful when we were intimate with each other. But I could not reveal my delight to anyone, not even to myself. Why was that?" Here is an example of the conviction that it is wiser not to reveal one's joy. "Today I would say that I felt guilty. My sister didn't have a boyfriend, and Father was against my having a boyfriend. Mother thought it was dangerous. I couldn't tell a soul. I couldn't share my joy with anyone." Think now for a moment of the little girl who had a circle of joy with her grandmother. She had not been able to tell anyone else about that circle, either, and she now felt guilty about a love that was her exclusive privilege. Her feelings of guilt prevented her from being able to show her joy.

Reconstructed biographies of joy can give us a great deal of valuable information. They show us how we express joy, and how our expressions of joy have changed with time. We gain insight into how we adapt ourselves to others to create a circle of joy. The dynamics of joy in our lives can serve to indicate major life transitions. But what is most important in my view is that the biography of joy can give us access to our own joy, joy — repressed from childhood — that might otherwise go unnoticed. I am searching not only for ways to understand the emotion of joy, but also for ways to awaken it.

PART III

Anatomy of Joy

7.

The Joy After and the Joy Before

By comparing the reconstructed biographies of joy collected from a number of people, I have been able to discover typical forms of joy. In this and the following two chapters, I will be using these forms to sketch an anatomy of joy.

The Joy After

The Swiss writer Max Frisch once wrote, "Happiness is consciousness set on fire. You will never forget this moment. You are like a film that has been exposed; memory will develop it later." Happiness is a form of joy, and "consciousness set on fire" is a wonderful expression for exposure to joy, that is, the perception of joy. Like a film that has been exposed and is yet to be developed, the meaning of a joyful experience becomes conscious much later, when memory develops what the perception exposed us to. For example, perhaps you spent a very pleasant week or evening with someone and then wrote that person a letter in the morning when you reached home, describing the beautiful experience. When you received a letter in return, the joy came alive in your memory once again. Clearly the memory of a joy is not more important than the perception of the joyful situation, since there would be nothing to remember if we did not first perceive it. Nonetheless, the memory of joy is also important in its own right.

Memory is the primary means by which we reconstruct our biographies of joy. What were you told as a small child about joy? Do you remember an early joy? We should let memories arise in the form of pictures, and search for situations in which we still have the sense of how delighted we were. The more genuine and existential our biography of joy becomes, the more we can live and reexperience these joys and the more they will bring wholeness.

The memory of joy develops the original moment of joy, as light develops an image on film. As this "consciousness set on fire" burns its way into our souls, it changes its shape. Our memory of joy reshapes our history of joy. Some people smooth out all the rough spots in their memories, leaving a story that offers nothing but delight. The events themselves were only half as joyful as the memory of them. When older persons start talking with glowing eyes about a marvelous event from their earlier years — the "good old days" — their loved ones will often add that time has contributed to the glow. But there are also those who further roughen the uneven spots in their memories, replacing their past joys with "yes, buts." This is a good way to kill all joy.

Anaïs Nin, in a book called *A Woman Speaks,* tells how she employed her memory of joy to help cure herself of cancer.

> Now I have a story I want to tell you. . . . In 1970 I had a touch of cancer and I was given radiation at the Presbyterian Hospital in New York for two weeks — six minutes each day. And I found myself in this dirty yellow room with a huge and very ugly machine in the middle. It was absolutely frightening, like something out of science fiction. You have to lie on the bed and they make a little drawing on your body where the radiation has to strike, and worst of

all the machine makes a terrible noise. So how was I going to deal with that? It was not so easy, but I decided that this machine was a projector and that I actually for six minutes was going to see the film of the loveliest, most happy and joyous days of my life. So as soon as the machine went on I closed my eyes and the film began, image after image of every place where I had been happy, every occasion, one after another. It was usually the sea and the beach and Tahiti and the south of France and Mexico. The landscape didn't change so very much but the situations did, and I was always choosing them. After six minutes when the noise stopped, the film would stop, and I would go home. The only worry I had was that I wouldn't have enough film, but the automatic continuity of the images got so real that at one point I was seeing myself driving down the road in the south of France and I was about to turn to visit Durrell, in my recollection, when I stopped myself and said: "I don't think I want to go that way, because I didn't have a very happy visit; I think I'll go the other way." So it went on, and I did have enough film to last the two weeks, six minutes a day, and I was completely cured. Now I am absolutely convinced that I helped the whole thing psychically. That's what I call magic. Because I haven't had any difficulty since.

So I wanted you to know that there isn't any occasion, there isn't any situation, where the psychic force of life, the love of life, and its joyousness can't somehow transport us and transfigure an event into one which we can recollect with pleasure [pp. 193–94].

This remarkable passage tells of a reconstructed biography of joy in the form of a film. I am always asked regarding my biographies of joy, "What about the unhappy times; can they be reconstructed, too?" The text just cited is a lively example of this, for undergoing radiation treatment is hardly a happy experience. And yet even in such a situation, it is possible to evoke the happiest times of our lives. Reconstructing a biography of joy makes it possible for us to feel joy again. It is essential to note that joy can directly influence our resistance to disease. It seems that we are more prepared to live when we recover our ability to be delighted.

THE JOY BEFORE

The anticipation of joy is to be distinguished from both the actual moment of joy and the memory of joy. The joy that comes from looking forward to something did not play a large role in the biography of the depressed woman that we examined. In other biographies of joy, the anticipation of joy is essential.

The joy before involves a high degree of expectation. "I expect it will be nice weather tonight. If not, I will be disappointed." Hope is much broader than expectation. Expectation is focused on a specific wish, which becomes the cause of disappointment if it does not materialize. Hope is a more expansive existential feeling, which sustains us and transcends specific expectations, as we will see. Not everyone can look forward to something to the same extent. We must be allowed time to do so, for if we are under stress we hardly have the chance to anticipate joy. Having something nice to look forward to is a cause of great delight.

The following example, from the biography of joy of an eighty-one-year-old man, illustrates some of the issues surrounding anticipated joy. I asked many older persons about joy, because a preconception exists—which I believe is false—that older people are less joyful than young people. It was March when I questioned this man. "Looking forward to something," he repeated, thinking my question over. "Yes, when I think now about how it will get warm again in May, then I can go into the garden and start planting, at my own speed. I can smoke a pipe and drink a glass of apple juice from time to time. I look forward to that a lot." I asked him what this joy felt like. "Very warm," he replied. "I can already feel the sun, and my heart is growing warm." Warmth is another quality typically associated with joy. Inspiration, an intense form of joy, is more readily associated with fire. "I have more things to look forward to now than I used to," he added spontaneously. "At my age, I have more time in general for joy." I then asked him what things he looked forward to when he was younger. When his father was getting ready to hand over the farm to him, he had a great deal to look forward to. When he made a long trip to Africa, he also had much to look forward to. "At my wedding, . . ." and he thought it over for a long time until his wife left the room, "I'm not so sure about that. There was a lot of joy, but also a lot of fear." Note the alliance of anticipated joy with dread. He then added that he never allowed himself to anticipate joy when the cows or the pigs were pregnant. He could only be glad after the brood had been born. There was too high a risk of being disappointed.

Dwelling in and nourishing itself on the future, the joy before is an uninhibited fantasy triggered by something to come. It is very close to longing, wishing, and expecting, hence the risk. The joy after is less subject to the danger of disappointment. Remembered joys are events of the past that we make present again. We have a basic supply of past experiences to feed our imaginations with. Although our memories of joy change shape in ways that we may not consciously control, we have even less control over our emotions surrounding an anticipated event, for there is much more room to imagine what we would like. I think it is clear what a great source of disappointment this can be.

I would like to share a simple example that deals with this risk. It concerns the anticipated joy of a fifty-three-year-old woman. "I always have something to look forward to on the evening before a celebration," she said, listing the many holidays that her family celebrated: Easter, Pentecost, birthdays, and so forth. "The part of it that I enjoy the most is when I prepare everything; I cook and I sing. My imagination runs rampant." I asked her about the content of her fantasies. "I imagine that my son-in-law and my own son finally stop fighting and get along, that there is a wonderful atmosphere, a feeling of belonging and togetherness, that our family has a heart and a soul. It sounds kitschy, but the thought just exhilarates me. Then I think about how my youngest daughter would be so happy that she would invite me to go with her on her next trip. I fantasize about such a lot of crazy stuff. I know it is fantasy, but as long as I continue the fantasy, I feel delighted and happy, and that's why I really only like the evening before a celebration, when I still have something to look forward to." I asked her what happens the next day. "Everything they do is only a pale reflection of what I had imagined."

This fantasized symbiosis is typical. I often use the expression "fantasized symbiosis" in the context of joy, because fantasies of anticipated joy are very often of a symbiotic nature. It is also typical that she would be disappointed the next day. She knew that her fantasy differed from reality, but she loved being carried away by such longings. She was a little unfair to her family, for how could she bring off a proper celebration when she was anticipating such spectacular joy? I do not think she gave her family much of a chance. I can see her saying the next morning, "And now comes the second part of the story."

There are writers who speak of magical joy in the context of anticipated joy [e.g., Izard, 1977]. They say that persons with magical joy often fear the envy of the gods. I would not describe this woman's joy as magical, because for me it would have to be much more compulsive and ritualistic to qualify as magic. When we work ourselves up to a state of anticipating joy, we are well aware that this is not reality, and that we will be coming back down to earth the next day. How do we deal with the disparity? It would not be meaningful to deprive this woman of her anticipated joy, because on the evening before she is truly happy, cooking with joy, and preparing for the celebration. I think her experience of delight is an essential part of her psychic housekeeping. I think she should enjoy this anticipated joy on the evening before, without worry, until she can enjoy it no more.

I said earlier that the joy before is very close to longing and to wishing. Our longings express themselves in our anticipation of joy. Often we discover in our longings things that we have not yet consciously admitted to ourselves. Our longings can carry new impulses from the unconscious into consciousness. If we were able to trust this function of our longings, we might be able to see more clearly what they want of us. For example, this woman might be able to say to herself, "I know what I would like to have happen. Tomorrow we will be together. What can be realistically expected? It is to be expected that my son-in-law and my own son will compete with each other." It is to be expected that the twenty-two-year-old daughter will not take her on that trip to Nepal. "Looking forward to the event is important and is a help to me," she might tell herself. "But what will happen tomorrow is something else again. I am going to try to put my dreams aside for now. They are meant only to inform me of what I would like from my family." It is important to tell ourselves in anticipation of a rendezvous, "Ah, so that is what I want deep down inside." Then we should be honest and ask ourselves, "What is really going to happen?" The joy before has the positive function of pulling us out of our everyday lives and endowing us with considerable psychic energy. But it represents a risk if we cannot distinguish between fantasy and realistic expectation.

Reconstructed biographies of joy bring us into contact with ourselves as creatures of joy. They indicate which joys are especially typical and significant for us. By means of our biographies of joy we also become conscious of problem areas that belong to our lives. And we gain insight into the manner in which joy is enhanced or spoiled in our lives, an insight that challenges us to discover how we enhance or spoil the joy of others.

8.

Making and Unmaking Joy

CAN JOY BE INDUCED?

GOETHE ONCE SAID, "It is enough to work; joy comes by itself."
I think this saying expresses a rather masochistic work ethic.
Is joy nothing more than a by-product of effort? Or is joy something that can be cultivated in its own right? We have observed
that joy can arise as a side-effect of a successful effort, or of
an apparently successful effort. From the outside, we often get
the impression of complete success, but if the person who did
the work has very high standards, he or she will invariably say,
"It is only half successful," cutting the joy in half. This is the
sort of joy that is a by-product of effort, with which we are
very familiar.

Joy can appear as a by-product, but it does not have to be
an *intended* by-product. There are many situations in which work
gives us joy without our ever thinking, "Now I am doing something so that I can experience joy." Joy arises when our work
takes on a life of its own, when we are sunk in thought and
stumble on a discovery, when we abandon ourselves to the
rhythm of some physical activity. Common to all these situations is deep concentration and commitment. It is not so much
the work or activity in itself, but rather the concentration and
presentness to ourselves that yields joy.

Can joy be stimulated? We have considered what the psychology of expression has to tell us about joy stimulated by joyful gestures. Actors abandon themselves to gestures of delight until they reach a point where it is impossible to distinguish joy that is acted from genuine joy. We noted that joy can be induced in persons who are somewhat suggestible. Then we took up the idea of joy by infection as treated in the text by Ingeborg Bachmann. By suggesting that ecstatic joy could be produced just by thinking about what a book would be like that would make us jump out of our skin with joy, Ingeborg Bachmann demonstrated that joy can be induced through the imagination.

Mass demonstrations afford another example of the contagious nature of emotions. The ease with which we can be infected partially accounts for the bad reputation that emotions enjoy. Aggression in a group is much more intense than aggression between two individuals, and collective anxiety goes far beyond what is normally experienced by one individual. Joy, like these other emotions, is also triggered by other persons, and can be highly infectious in groups — at rock concerts, for example, or on outings designed to create joy, such as a ski trip with a group of friends.

Let us now take a closer look at how joy is promoted through our upbringing. After that we will examine ways in which joy is ruined.

The Socialization of Joy

A recurrent question that found expression in the biographies of joy was, How is it that one person becomes more joyful and another less joyful? What does the upbringing and development of a joyful person look like in comparison with that of someone who is less joyful? Answers to these questions abound, even if they are indirect. We hear one answer whenever people say that they can present themselves more effectively when they meet with a joyful reception.

If a child says, "I can do anything," we can laugh and say, "You must be great if you can do anything!" Or we can say, "You will come back down to earth some day." Whether or not joy is reinforced depends on the reaction of others. The basic rule is that when children grow up in a joyful atmosphere, when joy is answered with joy, more joy will grow.

How joy is socialized is a question constantly raised by the theoreticians as well [Bollnow, 1955, 1956; Izard, 1977]. Many have observed that joy is not a product of human effort but rather a side-effect, sharing many characteristics with wonder, or interest. Much is known about the socialization and development of interest in a child [Izard, 1977]. The child's environment must be stimulating, but not too stimulating. Growing up in a complex family with a variety of persons, professions, interests, and hobbies is advantageous, but too much variety is a disadvantage. Poverty should not be too extreme, nor should wealth. It is known that certain age-specific interests are awakened by certain games, and that the threshold of a child's interest, like that of an adult, is very low. People, especially children, appear to be very full of wonder and very curious. The more curious—to use another word for wonder or interest— the parents are, the more curious the children will be as well. Much more is known about curiosity than about joy. It is known only that joy functions by means of infection. Children will become joyful in a joyful atmosphere.

There is also a theory that joy is genetically determined [Moser, 1978]. In this view, each individual is born with a given supply of joy; one person possesses greater potential and giftedness for joy than another. With regard to this view, it may be very illuminating to look at psychological theories in historical context. At first all problems were attributed to the trauma of birth. Later the first year of life suddenly became the decisive arena. Later still, everything was projected onto the first two years of life. Then suddenly the whole matter went intrauterine and pregnancy was given priority. At the moment everything is in the genes. It sometimes frightens me to think about genetic manipulation, for I wonder what we would do if a gene for emotion were discovered. Without settling the matter of the genetic bases for emotions definitively, I think it is safe to say that there are some persons who are more, and others who are less, prone to joy. Whether this difference can be attributed to the period of pregnancy, or whether it is already in the genetic material, is a matter that will probably be argued for centuries. Meanwhile, we can observe that certain people have a higher threshold for joy than others.

We do know that joy grows in children when it is reinforced. An interesting observation has been made in this regard. It has been determined that much less care is usually given to joyful, healthy children than to children who are ill, so many children learn that they must suffer in order to receive attention. "In order to get care, I have to be sick. When I am happy, nothing really happens." We often say to a joyful child, "If you're so happy, everything must be fine. Run along." It can be even worse, though; happy children can awaken envy.

When we stop to think about it, it is not obvious why we pay more attention to children who are not well than to those who are. If we want to have joyful human beings around us, we should encourage and stimulate children equally when they are happy. And we should give them the same amount of attention as a sign that their delight also brings us delight. I do not want to talk you out of caring for children who are ill. They need that. But perhaps they would get ill less often if they were also cared for when they were friendly and well-behaved and healthy.

Many biographies of joy witness to a creative delight that arises only when children are left to their own devices. "I remember how I used to play with pieces of wood and how I would build entire castles," reads a typical statement. "I made everything come alive with my imagination. It was really great and I felt like someone who rules over an entire empire and who can create this empire." Again we encounter the phenomenon of self-abandon: abandoning the self to play, to fantasy, to the process of giving shape. It is important for this play to be undisturbed.

Abandon can be disturbed by another child's interference. "Then my brother came along and ruined everything," reads a typical statement. One child plays with abandon, another child arrives, and envy takes its toll, as it does with adults, too. "He's playing so nicely; he is happy, and I have nothing."

Parents can also be very disturbing when they insist on cleaning up a room when children are at the peak of their play. I am sure there are mothers and fathers among my readers who are thinking, "You've got it backwards, Dr. Kast. Children play most intensely when they should be cleaning up." This may be true, but I still think we disrupt a child's self-forgetfulness more than we need to. We should ask ourselves if we are not envious of their ability to forget themselves. Creative tasks are fun if we can give ourselves over to them in self-forgetfulness.

Can joy be stimulated in childhood? Parents, as well as siblings and grandparents, who are capable of expressing joy definitely stimulate a child's joy. Joyful persons infect and reinforce each other in their joy. We can enhance joy deliberately by not taking joy for granted, but rather permitting ourselves to delight in a joyful child, and to accept the child's immersion in play.

CHILDLIKE JOY

An adult's sense of joy is often projected back into childhood. We tell ourselves that uninhibited joy was something we knew only as children. What for a child is uninhibited joy is experienced by an adult as a lack of emotional control. Behind this projection is the archetype of the child.

A fifty-year-old woman who reconstructed her biography of joy said, "I am much freer to take delight now than I was as a child; today I am more childlike in my joy." As she talked, she remained childlike in her expression. "I remember once as a small child I played in a puddle of water with my Sunday shoes and clothes on," she recalled. "The puddle was fairly deep and it made a nice splash. It was wonderful. I had the feeling everything was so full of life. I shrieked and got all wet. Then my older sister came and then my mother; she scolded me. I felt guilty, as if I were doing something wrong having such fun. Of course today I understand my mother very well. For me as a child, joy was always bound up with guilt or anxiety. Today I enjoy myself as I please. If I walk into a mud puddle, I wash my own clothes afterward." Joy is an emotion with consequences. The celebration of joy always leaves something to be cleaned up. Do you require permission to be joyful? Did you require permission as a child?

In the process of growing up, we learn that we must stop giving our emotions free rein. We seldom encounter adults who express their emotions without restraint. But recently I met with an eighteen-year-old disabled man who had absolutely no control over his emotions. He wanted me to be eighteen years old, too. When I told him I was not eighteen, he cried for a long time. Then he demanded that I call him on the telephone. "Yes, I will call," I promised. Then he asked two or three times, "Really? You'll call?" "Yes, really," I said; "I'll call." He was so glad, he almost fell out of his wheelchair, screaming out into the huge hall, "She'll call, she'll call, she'll call!" His father reprimanded him and he cried again. Here is an example of someone without any emotional control. To be an adult, we must have control over our emotions. We each have our methods. It could be that sometimes we are too heavy-handed, muffling our joy in accordance with an ideal that excludes noisiness.

The following example illustrates how uninhibited joy is not confined to our chronological childhood. A thirty-six-year-old woman told of how great joy had fallen to her over a broken leg. An adult girlfriend of hers had broken her arm, and this woman felt she must have a cast as well. She succeeded in breaking no less than her leg. "I can still see it," she recalled. "I have never been so delighted as I was when I got that cast. I was beaming with joy; there was no end to it." Occasions for joy are not always picturesque. Later we will see how joy can even be malicious.

Spoiling Joy

What aspects of our upbringing spoiled our joy? And how do we spoil the joy of ourselves and others? The answers to these two questions are closely related, since as a rule we unconsciously learned from our upbringing how to spoil joy.

The nature of joy draws on the mechanism of infection; we are happy when we can make others happy. Thus our joy is often spoiled when we express it to persons who are not gifted for joy, or who are in conditions or situations offering little occasion for joy, such as depression, preoccupation, or lethargy.

A lack of respect for the source of joy can kill it, especially among children. A child in high spirits, completely lost in some fantasy game, may be anxious to share his or her joy with the adults nearby. If the adults disregard this fantasy world, if they do not take it seriously, or if they fear that they have brought an unrealistic child into the world, the child will register their disapproval of the joy, and the joy will be transformed into shame, as if the child had been caught doing something wrong. Adults who disturb children in the midst of abandoned play also spoil their joy, as mentioned earlier. Such behavior on the part of adults indicates a repression of their own childlike qualities, which also explains why they cannot empathize very well with children.

As adults, we employ a similar method to spoil each other's joy: When we cannot share someone's joy, we express disapproval either of the person or of the joy. For example, one partner of a couple attends a public event and comes home enthusiastic, inspired, and happy. The other partner has sat at home, perhaps bored and certainly not inspired. The inspired partner raves about the event, with many repetitions. The partner who stayed home makes a disparaging remark, which bursts the bubble of joy. This process of killing joy is invariably born out of the inability of two persons to share a common source of delight. This inability may be due to the psychodynamics of the couple, to the inability of one partner to infect the other. The joyful partner may fail to convey enough substance, or may actually be demonstrating power through a show of having more joy.

A man once told me in a therapy session about an occasion when his wife spoiled his joy. One day he had completed his work well and had finished early. In a fine mood, he bought a bouquet of flowers on his way home, which he brought to his wife, telling her without apology about the fine job he had done. Greeted with a face growing longer, he finally asked her, "Aren't you glad that I'm home already?" "Well, you know," she answered, "you have such a wonderful time. I fight it out here with the kids. No one sees the work I do. You can come home and be the king. You beam with joy, and you even have enough energy left over for flowers. I'm here all the time, so small and ugly. And now I'm spoiling your evening, too." This sad but common encounter illustrates how a good mood, rather than being infectious, can arouse envy. She could have let herself be infected by joy, and there would still have been time for something to come of the evening. Instead, she said in effect, "You have it and I don't. Poor me, the victim." Joyful persons make an easy target for guilt under this sort of attack. They seem to be culpable according to an unwritten law that says "Thou shalt not outshine thy neighbor." It is very difficult to keep our joy from crumbling when it is disparaged by others.

Delight in the joy of another person is grounds for celebration. But celebration of another's joy means being able to accept the fact that she or he has an emotion which we ourselves would like to have. We often try to deal with this by turning the joy of another person into our own joy. For example, if a colleague wins a prize, you may be a bit envious. You are invited to a celebration. You tell yourself, "At least it's great that one of us got the prize." This is how we deal with envy, so that we can share another's joy in spite of it. If envy has spoiled vicarious joy and a gesture of joy is attempted anyway, the gesture will generally fail to kindle enthusiasm.

The excitement that accompanies joy and inspiration, along with the experience that every joy must subside after reaching a high point, often produces a prematurely cautious attitude, like that expressed in the saying that pride goes before a fall. This attitude may have more to do with envy than with wisdom. Feelings of elation cause envy. "You can laugh now," someone may say to a happy child, "but wait till you grow up and have to carry the load I carry." Or there is the remark also heard among adolescents, "Go ahead and laugh while you can," meaning "What you are doing is incredibly immature."

The joy that is derived from success and competence is spoiled not only by others' envy, but also by our own false ideal of humility, which children are indoctrinated with by inconsistent methods of education and upbringing. They are expected to be independent, competent, smart, and so forth, and yet they should not know that they are, or at least should not behave as if they knew it. True humility is the awareness that we can always go beyond ourselves, and that we exist within the greater context of life as a whole. Humility means knowing our place within all of creation; it does not mean devaluing the feelings that give us a sense of joy and worth.

The spoiling of joy is intimately related to shame; when our joy is dampened or entirely prevented, we tend to react with shame. We feel annihilated, and to protect our sense of self-worth we nourish vengeful feelings. Joy thwarted leads to a whole array of unhappy emotions associated with our shadow, but joy itself has a shadow side as well.

9.

The Shadow Side of Joy

MALICIOUS JOY

A THIRTY-YEAR-OLD MAN told about preparing for a walking contest together with a friend. When the friend suffered a fatigue fracture in his foot, the man confessed, "a deep joy took hold of me. When I heard of his fracture, I immediately organized a celebration for my friends, including my injured partner. The party went on into the night, because on the next day there would be no training, no slavery, nothing." Though he was highly pleased that the friend had received what he felt was a just reward for his excessive ambition, he was deeply disturbed by his own malicious joy. "I have seldom experienced such a wonderful sense of joy," he soberly admitted. "I had the feeling that life had really done me a good turn. On the other hand, I felt very warped and wrongheaded. 'What kind of jerk are you,' I asked myself, 'to be so delighted by this poor fellow's misfortune?'"

He thought there was no such thing as malicious joy. This attitude provoked my own malicious joy, for I am glad when people who are so proper find out that they are human beings like the rest of us. You can see that malicious joy also has a cumulative effect.

How are we to understand the psychodynamics of this man's

malicious joy? Perhaps the relationship between the two men was based on competition; when one could go no farther, the other would say, "You're not pooping out already, are you?" In this case the fatigue fracture granted them respite from a very stressful competition, and was a sign that their competition had been excessive. Perhaps they had a rather strenuous relationship, the kind in which they kept score with each other, driving one to the point where he could celebrate the injury of the other.

I said at the outset that joy is an emotion of harmony, that joy falls to those whose lives are back in tune. It is also conceivable that this man wanted a different kind of relationship with his friend, that he wanted their relationship to be more balanced, more in tune. In their relationship, joy and cruelty, to put it bluntly, may have been allied in sadistic joy. Joy is not always just elevating; base motives can lie below these heights.

I believe that everybody gloats, although people did not mention joy of a malicious sort very often in their reconstructed biographies. It is forbidden to gloat, which explains why we behave as if we did not—behavior that does not help matters, since joy over the misfortunes of others exists whether we admit it or not. In gloating we see the interaction of joy and cruelty, which is very close to sadism. Sadism shows us that the emotion of joy has two sides. Joy involves not only solidarity and connection, but also the total domination over another person or torture of another person. It is not clear where malicious joy ends and sadism begins.

I would like to provide two more short examples of malicious joy in order to move you to discover your own. This is my own shadow of joy, I know. But I believe that it is better to face the things we wish were not there: it lessens their control over us.

An eighteen-year-old female student reported: "I have a friend at school who always gets such damned good grades. And now she just gave a presentation that the teacher didn't like at all, especially not its political implications. The teacher criticized her sharply. I was so glad. I was happy for two days. I sang, and my mother asked me if I was in love. I felt good about myself, really good. Oh, I know you are not supposed to gloat, but I couldn't help it; it was so good for me. The only thing that irritates me is that she didn't suffer at all from the defeat." Perhaps you have similar memories from your own school days.

Malicious joy does not distinguish between young and old or male and female. A sixty-six-year-old man told me, "I have a neighbor here who is so 'above it all,' always acting as though she were better than everyone else. Now just imagine: She has to move into a retirement home. Yes, seventy-one and she has to go to the old folks' home. Usually I don't like hearing about someone who has to go to an old folks' home: It reminds me that I may have to go too some day. But in this case I was delighted. That snobby old bitch has to go to the old folks' home. She doesn't have it any better than anyone else; there's justice in the world after all."

It is typical that this man's malicious joy was instigated by someone described as being "above it all." People who elicit malicious joy are usually seen as better than average, especially talented, hardworking, or arrogant. Envy is involved. Their presumed sense of superiority may sometimes be more projection than reality, though. If we fail to live out a talented part of ourselves — working and risking less by remaining mediocre — our talents are repressed, and so we project them onto other persons who represent a challenge to us because they make our problem visible and tangible. Reminding us that we could be there too, they are like a thorn in our flesh that must somehow be extracted. We assume they act superior whether they really do or not.

This aging man was happy to know that there is justice in the world after all. "No one has it better than anyone else," he might have said to himself; "The gods have no favorites." This would confirm his own worth and position in life. At least in comparison with the woman who was "put in her place," he would be better off. Obviously such gloating is rooted in competitive thinking and envy. Self-esteem, which is connected with joy, here derives from comparison, rather than self-assurance. We are raised to think competitively. As small children, we were always compared with each other. Who is bigger? Who is faster? Who can do better? This constant evaluation by comparison with others played a huge role in our upbringing. The results are disastrous: Our sense of personal worthiness does not come from self-acceptance, but rather from external approval. If I complete a task, it does not really matter if someone else could do it better or worse. It is I who am completing the task. If I have the feeling that it is right for me, I have a good feeling about doing it. But if I start thinking that there is someone in the world who can do it better, my good feeling and joy may break down. The thought "But couldn't someone else have done it better?" is probably the most common way of killing joy. Furthermore, then I have to make sure that no one *can* do it better, so I belittle others, often decreasing their joy too.

Rivalry has a place in a person's development that should not be denied. When we behave competitively, we draw the boundaries between ourselves and others in order to become unique individuals. Sibling rivalry gives children the chance to feel their strength and their limits so that they can know and become themselves. Rivalry is only problematic when it becomes a law of life. Then rivalry changes the nature of joy or even leads to malicious joy.

And yet joy, on the other hand, offers the possibility of overcoming a certain rivalry. At its peak, joy is the emotion that can help us overcome rivalry. Huge rivalries prevent joy; but robust joy can overcome competitive thinking, which otherwise seems never to end.

Although malicious joy is very close to sadism, it has the advantage of not being direct like sadism but instead of being detached, once removed. We have not inflicted the suffering; fate has. If we behave sadistically, we have to take responsibility for the suffering we inflict, unless we are sadistic voyeurs who take vicarious delight in the sadistic behavior of others. In malicious joy we can say with relief, "I didn't do the evil deed; somebody else did it; fate did it." We can simply enjoy the fact that somebody has had a bad time, without suffering from a guilty conscience, at least not right away. Later our morality makes us feel guilty, since we believe that malicious joy should hardly exist. A little malicious joy is allowed, but not too much.

SADISM

Sadism is defined as a feeling of pleasure or joy that comes from inflicting suffering on another person, either in fantasy or in fact. Sadism may or may not be combined with sexuality. It involves fantasies of total domination over another human being, having them at our disposal, bringing them to the point of capitulation. Its themes are mastery and submission, pain and torture. Torture is a means of proving that another human being is subject to our own will, impotent, and defenseless. Sadism is destructive and inhuman because it denies the autonomy of others, forcing them to forfeit their free will. Human dignity requires a certain degree of self-determination, so sadism is destructive of human dignity.

The psychodynamic root of sadism is a will to mastery. Ranging from a grandiose self to a destructive god, the self-image of a sadist seems to assure absolute domination over others.

Cowering behind this facade, though, is someone who feels utterly unworthy and insufficient. Sadism offers the chance to feel good in spite of inferiority, and joy arises from the interplay and merging between aggressor and victim. But since merging produces anxiety as well as joy, a demarcation is needed, and this is provided by the division of roles between torturer and tortured.

Sadistic persons derive joy not from creating something new; they derive their joy from destruction. They do not receive joy from being interpersonally related in a healthy way. Nor can they wait for a stroke of good fortune. They are not active persons in a creative sense; Erich Fromm repeatedly emphasized that destruction is one way out of passivity. They can feel their strength when they destroy something. They can probably even feel their strength more directly in an act of destruction than in a creative act. The consequences of such an act are another matter.

Destruction can create the feeling of being in agreement with oneself, which explains the joy that it affords as well as the threat that it poses. Since this self-assurance does not last long, new targets for destructive acts are continually sought, so that one soon enters a spiral of destruction. It is much easier to get sucked into a spiral of destruction than a spiral of joy. The grandiose self compensates with the feeling of being powerful and able to rule over others. Feeling powerful, sadists find self-acceptance, and yet their dependence on the counterpart continues. The good feeling does not persist, and its disappearance results in a spiral of sadism. We need to realize that destructiveness as well as creativity can be a source of joy, that sadism also generates solidarity, and that destructive behavior can even degenerate into an orgy of joy and elation. Sobriety and shame over what was destroyed in the joyous ecstasy of destructive rage may arrive only in retrospect, if at all.

Sadistic joy partakes in all the general features of joy already described. Sadistic joy is also an emotion that binds people together. Sadistic tortures often take place in groups, where joy seems to reach a high pitch. Any feelings of guilt that might arise are split off and delegated to the victims: "It is their fault." Sadism usually stands in the service of an idea such as, "We have to drive the devil out of you so that you will finally be happy again. If you want to become a good person again, I'm afraid I'm going to have to punish you quite severely." Sadistic acts always stand under the banner of some "good," and the joy issuing from their performance has an elating effect.

The difference between sadistic joy and creative joy is noticeable, though, when the moment of joy has become a memory. The memory of creative joy gives us an elated feeling, whereas the memory of sadistic joy makes us feel guilty and ashamed once it becomes at all conscious. This consciousness subjects the ego to renewed stress and a feeling of unworthiness, forcing it to summon the aid of the grandiose self to invent new tortures. A circle of sadism is set in motion when guilt and shame enter consciousness. There are many people who react sadistically and are never aware of it. They "educate," or "devote themselves to the good of the human race." One has the impression that they feel virtually chosen to remake humankind into something better than it really is. The sadistic component of such a sentiment goes unnoticed. Such people are often quite subtle sadists.

Subtle sadism can also take on collective proportions; I would like to address one form of this subtle sadism, because it is an obstacle to joy. Many people say, "Do I have the right to rejoice when everything is so bad in the world?" I have also heard this subtle form of sadism expressed in a slightly different way: "Not only do you speak about joy, you even take shameless delight in it. Meanwhile the world is coming apart at the seams."

Less subtly stated, a sadistic commandment lurks in the background: "Thou shalt not rejoice," as if to imply that only a disgraceful human being is capable of rejoicing. When we think of how vitalizing joy actually is, this desired prohibition of joy because of the terrible state of the world actually proves to be sadistic.

Subtle sadism is usually smuggled in under the banner of some cause. If we are going to save the world, let us do so out of joy rather than the prohibition of joy on account of the sad state of the world. Nothing has ever been saved out of depression but only out of a passionate love for life. Passionate love does not want to destroy; at worst it wants to devour. Nor is it psychologically correct to declare, "One should not rejoice given the terrible state of the world." There have been very trying situations in which joy glimmered through intense pain and suffering like a fleeting patch of blue in a gray sky: "Ah yes, life can feel like this, too." We are outraged by brutal sadists, but we need to keep an eye out for the subtle sadists as well.

The Grandiose Self

In the context of sadism, the grandiose self affords a fleeting experience of something like joy. In Jungian psychology we use the expression "grandiose ego complex" [Kast, 1990]. The grandiose self represents a stage of ego identity in early childhood. Normally when we speak of the self, we are dealing with ego development and identity. When we speak of the Self in the Jungian sense, we go far beyond ego identity. "Grandiose self" and "ideal self" refer to issues of ego identity and the ego complex.

The grandiose self denotes a stage in early childhood development when children have the feeling they can do anything; they are omnipotent, all-knowing, and all-powerful. Children need to go through this developmental stage, which is facilitated by parental mirroring. Children are mirrored by repeatedly hearing that they are good, nice, strong, wonderful, and important as independent personalities. The first effect of such mirroring is the development of a healthy grandiose self, which connects with what I said earlier about the development of joy: If we take delight in mirroring, the child's self-acceptance and self-esteem will be more effectively enhanced than if we mirror the child because psychologists say we should.

Recently I saw a parent in the act of mirroring who made me curse psychology. The child asked, "Wasn't I great?" The parent responded, flatly, "Yes, you were great, just wonderful." There was more emotion expressed in my writing about this than there was in the voice of that child's parent. One could just as well have played a tape. This is not mirroring; mirroring is letting oneself get caught up by the child's emotion and taking real delight in it.

Around the third year of life, the child's grandiose self-image becomes relativized. The child begins to realize, "I am not omnipotent, all-knowing, or all-powerful, but there must be others who are." By idealizing and identifying with parents and other relations, the child remains a little omnipotent and a little all-knowing. Rather than speaking of the grandiose self at this stage, we now refer to the processes of idealization and identification. With time, idealization gives way to the development of a so-called ideal self, and idealization and identification become intrapsychic dynamics. Although based on reality, the ideal self is still slightly elevated above the real self, as if to say, "Aside from this and that, I couldn't be much better."

The ideal self should make us relatively independent of praise and reproach, with the emphasis on *relatively*, since identity remains very susceptible to damage. Any major stress poses a threat to one's identity. A person who has not been able to go through the development just outlined, and who is not capable of repeating the phases of such a development, may have a very difficult time and may regress to a previous stage in order to reactivate the grandiose self of early childhood, which makes us feel omnipotent, all-knowing, and all-powerful again.

Problematic situations reactivate the grandiose self, either intrapsychically or through the idealization of some important person. This reactivation produces a momentary effect similar to that of joy. Joy influences our ego complex, our experience of integrity, and our feeling of self-acceptance and self-confidence so that we can accept the world and ourselves. Letting down our guard, we feel vital, energetic, and relaxed. Joy could replace regression back to the grandiose self—if only joy could be produced at will. Unfortunately, in a threatening situation it is not possible to summon joy. However, we need to appreciate that it is always there; albeit at times of overwhelming stress, joy is immersed in the sea of the unconscious.

PART IV

Inspiration

10.

The Existential Meaning of Mania

BOISTEROUSNESS, CHEERFULNESS, AND HAPPINESS are exhilarating, infectious, and irresistible. A manic psychosis confronts us with an imbalance in which the mood is inordinately buoyant, with an exaggerated cheerfulness put on display. Thinking gets carried away, with a pursuit of new ideas, many of which are immediately put into practice. Manically unstable persons suffer from a compulsive urge to be active and from a heightened drive that can hardly be slowed. Their exuberance is often fueled by self-overestimation and grandiosity [Bleuler, 1966]. They feel happy, rejuvenated, filled with boundless strength. Their euphoria can turn into rage if their urge to be active is frustrated by obstacles. Bleuler wrote (p. 411) that even though manic persons have a very agitating effect on the psychiatric ward, it is possible to have good rapport with them—"as with badly trained children of whom one is fond." I have yet to encounter anyone who says bad things about manic persons; a certain envy is more common. I have heard many bad things said about schizophrenics, and I have heard downright cruel things said about depressive persons.

In a recent handbook on psychiatry, Tölle [1986] points out that although manic persons can be jolly, they can also be thoroughly tense and irritating. Nevertheless, I think we tend to idealize this instability, which possesses so many qualities we would like to call our own if only we could have them without being unstable: joy, enthusiasm, ecstasy, heightened drive. The inspired state that so many people long for is visible in mania, if in a distorted and thus both fascinating and fearful form.

Manic persons are extremely active and nearly exempt from fatigue, constantly busy and on the move. They exhaust everyone else, requiring no rest and refusing to go to bed because of their substantial lack of inhibition. It appears that they enter easily into relationships, but it is more accurate to say they have no capacity for distance. They are capable of throwing themselves at others and making demands they would never dream of making if they were not in a manic phase.

The Greek word *mania* means frenzy, rage, or madness, but also enthusiasm. The god of mania is Dionysus. Soon we will devote more attention to Dionysus, as the god of ecstasy. What we are now considering as a pathological picture expresses a widespread human longing, the longing to go beyond all limits.

The physician Ernst Kretschmer and the existential analyst Ludwig Binswanger were both highly interested in the human meaning of mania. Kretschmer [1951] wrote about cyclothymia and character, and Binswanger [1955] made an existential analysis of manic patients.

CYCLOTHYMIA

Manic-depressive illness falls under the psychiatric designation of cyclothymia. Kretschmer's description of the cyclothymic temperament made its way into popular speech with the phrase "Happy as heaven, sad as Styx" (Himmelhoch jauchzend, zu Tode betrübt). This phrase occurs in a poem by Goethe, who was probably the most famous historical figure with a cyclothymic character. Kretschmer translated cyclothymia as "circular madness" (Kreiswütig). Cyclothymic states, he argued, could be experienced by a totally normal ego, by a neurotic ego, or by a poorly structured ego complex. He saw cyclothymia as an attitude and disposition that could become manic-depressive psychosis at its extreme. Cyclothymia denotes a cycle of happiness and unhappiness. Colloquially we speak of "ups and downs." While on the "up" side of the cycle, cyclothymic persons are elated, sunny, inclined to be in a good mood, a bit foolish, humorous, and funny. They give the impression that they possess a bottomless well of strength, though they may also seem a bit too driven. On the "down" side, they are melancholic, ponderous, withdrawn, depressed, and silent. Nothing can delight them and, if insulted, they are saddened rather than enraged. The attitude of cyclothymia as a whole rotates, so that states of adventurous euphoria turn into darker, less productive moods. Many artists and creative persons have cyclothymic temperaments, as do entire geographical areas. The inhabitants of the Swiss Alps, commented Kretschmer, are generally cyclothymic, and the music from that region is pervaded by a euphoric-melancholic quality. We could include nearly all of Switzerland in this description.

Cyclothymia implies the coexistence of "ups" and "downs" in a single emotional cycle. Thus melancholic elements lurk behind the euphoric moods, and when melancholic persons thaw out again they can be extraordinarily cheerful and humorous. We tolerate extreme emotional oscillation in someone who is falling in love, but otherwise we tend to consider someone who is "happy as heaven, sad as Styx" pathological.

Kretschmer observed that it is characteristic for the cyclothymic person to be very responsive, especially during the manic phase, but that this responsiveness has no great durability. Thus it stands to reason that joy and superficiality have something in common.

Cyclothymic persons tend to fly off the handle, but do not

hold grudges. They are related to their fellows, and are helpful by nature rather than by principle. (Kretschmer seems to have found helpfulness by nature and not by principle almost blameworthy.) Such persons are gregarious, have a thirst for action, and love to work. They are headstrong but not tenacious because as they continue through the emotional cycle they will again reach the low side when they will be disinclined to follow through with projects or commitments they have undertaken on the high side. In the absence of endurance, toughness, and firmness, foolhardiness is likely to take root. In Kretschmer's views on cyclothymia, it is noticeable that a great deal more attention is given to the manic than to the depressive phase. Moreover, a definite prejudice is apparent as well: Whoever goes through life being so jolly can never be profound. We can restrict Kretschmer's descriptions to psychopathology, or we can leave them as general categories of human experience, as he did.

HYPERTHYMIA

"Cyclothymia" literally means a cycle (*kyklos*) of temperament (*thymos*), whereas "hyperthymic" means literally excessive (*hyper*) temperament (*thymos*). Hyperthymia was once classified as a psychopathy, but this term is no longer used, and the phenomenon is now explained as a problem in the structure and formation of the self. Like a cyclothymic person, someone with a hyperthymic constitution is also described as being elated and having a superficially cheerful basic mood that is practically indistinguishable from an untouchable optimism; unlike cyclothymics, hyperthymics do not regularly experience a depressive phase. Cyclothymic persons know the night side of being, and yet rise in the morning to see the sun again. Hyperthymic persons split off their dark side, staying in a happy mood around the clock; having a lively temperament, they can be talkative and zealously active. Hyperthymia serves to fend off anxiety and depression cheerfully, optimistically, and invulnerably, with the aid of the grandiose self, as if to say, "I am so great that I can dissociate and defend myself against depression and anxiety. Other persons may have them, but not I."

The attitude adopted by the grandiose self lacks relatedness. Relatedness is an important attribute of joy, in my view, even if it is sometimes enacted on a relatively primitive, undifferentiated level. Usually persons with a hyperthymic constitution are not related to others; they are too highly self-centered. Triumphs, for example, may be announced without the least display of concern for others. I once saw a man in therapy who had no qualms about telling his wife for an hour and a half how terrific he was. Occasional identification with something great is tolerable, but anything more triggers a negative reaction in others. For the grandiose self, there is no more relatedness, nor is there a desire to share joy; instead there is an alliance of joy and power: "I'm glad I have it and you don't."

THE MANIC TRIAD

Today mania is defined as belonging to cyclothymia as well as hyperthymia; one must distinguish between Kretschmer's older and Tölle's newer description. In general, cyclothymia means melancholy and mania, manic-depressive disease, or affective psychosis. Mania exhibits the so-called manic triad, consisting of elevated mood, heightened drive, and flight of ideas. In the manic triad we see a direct relation with the hyperthymic constitution, which is also called hypomania.

Someone under the influence of a flight of ideas, a typical disturbance of thinking, cannot stop talking or writing and leaps from one topic to the next, getting lost in trivialities. I once had an analysand who was basically depressive. Suddenly a manic phase erupted in him during which within seventy-two hours he wrote 250 typewritten pages about the revision of teaching practices. He did not sleep, and parts of what he had written were quite good. There were some very odd pages, but they were not simply nonsense, and there were some very good passages as well. He also called me several times during the night—the first time at 11:00 P.M., with a good idea, then again at 3:00 A.M., when I was asleep, and again at 5:00 A.M., when I was irritated at being disturbed. "Don't you do anything besides sleep?" he asked. This is an example of being attacked by someone who is exempt from fatigue. A linguistic aspect of the inability to stop talking that is a feature of this disturbance is the stringing together of words with only a loose semantic, and sometimes only a tonal, association.

The flight of ideas involves a huge overestimation of oneself attributable, in psychodynamic terms, to the grandiose self. Immersed in a flight of ideas, manic people believe that they are highly intelligent, and there are no problems in the world they cannot solve. They make revolutionary inventions and may even get as far as the patent office. Some individuals also embark on totally unrealistic financial undertakings during a flight of manic ideas. In these connections we speak of an expansive mania. The man who wrote the 250 pages was a fanatic bicyclist. On a single afternoon he bought fifteen wheels, one after the other. He kept thinking that the next wheel would be better than the last. He ran out of money and got himself into debt.

Perhaps you can sense the unique dynamic of this kind of elation, which turns into a possession and a frenzy. Persons in such a state have no insight into the morbid character of their behavior, and without reflecting, they put their ideas very quickly into practice. A manic state can have the effect of heightening self-esteem, but it is truly grandiose and therefore makes it agonizing to meet constantly with dull but reasonable responses from the world. When I began to read a few pages written by the reformer and fanatic bicyclist, he quickly became exasperated. "You read so slowly!" he exclaimed. "You should be finished by now." In comparison with him, the world was dense, annoying, and incomprehensible.

After the manic phase subsides, some persons are pleased with what they have done. Others find it embarrassing, still others unbearable. In mania the grandiose self takes control of the ego, which is rendered helpless and void. By contrast, in creative ecstasy, as we shall see, the ego is seized by other contents of the unconscious, and rather than being possessed or obliterated it becomes permeable.

BINSWANGER ON MANIA

Ludwig Binswanger, the phenomenological psychoanalyst, attempted to describe the existential feeling residing in mania. In an article entitled "The Anthropological Meaning of High-flownness," Binswanger posed the question of why our aspiring to the heights can turn into high-flownness. Why do we suddenly find ourselves out on a limb? You recall that we have not yet answered a similar question about joy. When does joy grow hollow or begin to falter instead of continuing to rise? Why does it reach a point of collapse? What, similarly, is the limit to high-flownness?

Binswanger proposed a simple and fascinating idea. He suggested that we must live both vertically and horizontally, and that a balance must be struck by which we allow ourselves to be carried up into the heights only as far as we stride into the distance. Striding into the distance would mean a venture of gathering experience, using insight and foresight to broaden our field of vision and to take hold of the world. This horizontal dimension of human life involves making distinctions, collecting knowledge, and processing it. It involves working through an insight and working it out in our lives. In the vertical dimension, we long to be carried up and away on the wings of elated moods, accompanied by passion and the power of the imagination. By overcoming gravity, we are lifted above the pressure of anxiety and everyday life, to where we can gain an overall view of things, a higher insight.

Apparently it is a human need to overcome gravity. This mild form of mania, bordering on ecstasy—what I am calling joy—is sought in fasting, meditation, intoxication, drugs, and other ways. Binswanger's concept of the human balance accounts for the problem of losing groundedness when we try to go too high: If height and breadth grow out of proportion, and if we go higher still, we become high fliers without any ground control. The human balance can also be disturbed by going too far in the dimension of breadth, which could be visualized as getting bogged down. Height and breadth must be in the right proportion. When we go too high, our return to reality and balance inevitably takes the form of sinking or falling.

According to Binswanger, human beings are material and subject to the trials of this world, but through love they can take part in something transcendent. High-flownness sets a limit on joy, for it emphasizes the danger of holding on to joy too long. Having experienced the injury and hardship of reorientation after a fall, we are wary of embarking on another flight of joy. The manic form of life evades such considerations, which belong to the dimension of breadth, preferring to stay aloft.

Binswanger saw mania in images of skipping, leaping, and floating, motions associated with dance, which he called "the movement of presentness." For the manic the dimension of height takes precedence over that of breadth in dance. Mania can be visualized as a dancer who is spatially overextended. It can be quite a nuisance when someone on the dance floor claims much more space than is occupied by his or her body alone. However, if a dancer becomes too preoccupied with counting steps, he or she will likely not be carried up into the heights of ecstasy, remaining instead a prisoner in the dimension of breadth. (The overextension of the grandiose self is also something we sometimes experience when we drive an automobile and through it occupy an enlarged bodily space.)

Binswanger saw the heart of the maniacal form of life as a festive, unreflective joy in being. It is difficult not to idealize someone who naively affirms being, celebrates the multivalence of life, and believes wholeheartedly in activity. Life for such a person is no heavy burden; it flies, and there is no end of things to be discovered; nor is there any limit to a person's potency. For those who lack a festive spirit or who are poor in ideas, mania is especially alluring. And the flight of ideas is very close to creative thinking. Binswanger observed that scientists make use of manic states. Brainstorming, for example, develops out of a flight of ideas and functions on that basis.

The essence of mania is a never-ending celebration of being, any disruption of which results in anger. Binswanger described manics as flighty, contagious, and infectious, but also as intolerant of opposition, which throws them into fits of rage. Dwelling exclusively in the present, manics abandon everything of historical value, and they cannot be taken at their word, because that would mean commitment.

Binswanger observed that the approach of the climax to a festival of joy includes disintegration and the presence of death. This is true of individual as well as collective states of mania. For example, the carnival season (Mardi Gras or the Swiss Fasnacht) is not only a time of gaiety but also of death. It is interesting to note how many depressing things happen when manic persons participate in a celebration. The end of a manic state can be tragic, comprising anything from disintegration to complete immobility. It is like the extinction of a firework.

Nevertheless, there is a fine line between joyous optimism and mad optimism and madness. Binswanger cited Goethe, who wrote of the close connection between inspiration and madness: "I never believed there was anything to attain. I always thought I already had it. They could have crowned me, and I would have thought no explanation was necessary. And yet precisely because of this I was just a human being like the next. All that distinguished me from a foolish madman was my quest to work through with my own powers what had deeply stirred me, to earn with my own merit what I had received." Goethe's inspiration fell short of madness because he exerted himself in the dimension of breadth, through work. I think that rootedness is just as important as work. To protect ourselves against the perpetual decline and fall of joy, we must be rooted. Binswanger concluded by saying, "Merely festive joy in being leads to madness. But a purely problematic encounter with being — melancholy—leads to death." In the final analysis, we need a balance of both elating and grounding emotions—and this, after all, leads to creative play and work, embodying the endless paradox of death and rebirth.

II.

Ecstasy, Inspiration, and Creativity

ONE OFTEN HEARS the complaint that today's world knows no ecstasy. The loss of religious avenues to ecstasy has left a vacuum that we attempt to fill with everything from soccer matches to sex, from fasting to dancing, from meditation to jogging. Our present fitness craze has less to do with health—actually I believe it is fairly unhealthy—than with our longing for increased energy and drive. We attempt to stay fit in order to be poised for ecstasy. There are better ways, it seems to me.

Music often transmits an elevated mood; we may listen to loud music to revitalize ourselves and increase our energy. Extended periods of repetitive movement can be very effective in producing an ecstatic effect. Shamans transport themselves into ecstasy by means of drumming, chanting, and dancing. We can stimulate ourselves by going on a flight of ideas. Certain books mediate a wealth of ideas, into which we can plunge to enrich our own supply. We can also allow ourselves to be influenced and animated by persons who are overflowing with ideas. It is maddening how few really inspired and ecstatic individuals we actually encounter. They often lock themselves away in seclusion.

According to one theory, people today find themselves resigned and depressed because they mistakenly think they should constantly be inspired. But I believe that we suffer from a real loss of inspiration itself, especially religious inspiration, which has been supplanted by a number of secular alternatives. When all else fails, we resort to the use of intoxicating substances in our attempt to fulfill the need for ecstasy. We basically risk our lives in order to feel alive. The heightened drive together with the richness of ideas characteristic of ecstasy is probably the very highest existential feeling that can be attained, the pinnacle of all peak experiences. Intoxication, ecstasy, and creativity offer us ways to leap over the limits of concrete experience and established, everyday realities. These elated emotions answer our need to transform ourselves into persons who are more alive, who are involved, who have the energy to act, who believe in change and, finally, who hope.

To be inspired, extending ourselves out into the world as far as we soar up to the heights, is to live creatively. Goethe suggested that to speak of inspiration means to speak of creativity — creativity as the possibility of turning a mood, feeling, or idea into a concrete reality. The present craze about creativity in psychology bespeaks a hope that creativity can transform an existential mood into a reality. I do not mean artistic creativity, though I do not mean to exclude it either, but rather a general existential creativity, that is, creativity at the level of the personality.

A popular saying about creativity, probably attributable to Goethe, defines creative work as consisting of 5 percent inspiration and 95 percent perspiration. These are not very pleasing proportions. The point is that inspiration must be brought back down into life again; otherwise we are high-flown without any connection to the ground of reality. We all know people who possess a wealth of wonderful ideas, but never get around to making them real. Such persons are often told that they are lazy. I believe they are simply too busy chasing after the next idea, so that they never write down their thoughts or pass them along to someone else. In their desire to experience more of the inspiration that makes them feel so alive, they have not yet understood that perspiration can also make them feel very alive — the moment when an idea takes form and becomes real. It does one inestimable good to sink into a grandiose fantasy about the "idea of the century." This good feeling belongs to the play phase of creativity. But later when a pale reflection of the original idea lies before us in black and white, we can be filled with another equally good feeling.

In the creativity literature, a great deal is said about how creativity is accompanied by joy, enthusiasm, and inspiration. The American creativity researchers May [1853], Rosner and Abt [1972], Taylor [1964], Maslow [1962], and Anderson [1959], are unanimous in their conviction that joy is the emotion produced by a peak experience of creative self-realization, which is equivalent to inspiration. Or they say that creativity is the highest expression of self-esteem, the summit of existential feeling and life in general. This is not to overlook the anxiety always lurking in the background of creativity: fear of not being able to create, of making mistakes, and of being rejected. Since anxiety silences the creative act, everything that takes form through creativity represents a triumph of vitality over fear. Creativity consists of a struggle between two impulses, one that would carry us up into the heights, and another that would put us to work in the zone of gravity.

There is much discussion in the literature about an organized versus an inspired approach to creativity, but I do not think these approaches can be so clearly divided, for even someone who approaches creativity in a very structured way must at some point wait for a good idea, and so depends on inspiration. Most creativity researchers agree that inspired ideas emerge from the unconscious. They seize, stir, and take possession of us, posing the radical demand that they be given form. Highly creative persons are stirred more deeply than less creative persons, experience a more unconditional demand, and have a more refined capacity for giving form to what has moved them. The secret of creativity is the ability to let oneself be gripped by the unconscious.

Earlier I wrote of joy in terms of surrender. Inspiration, too, involves surrender to the complexes and archetypes constellated in the unconscious. Our capacity for such surrender is determined as much by our individual life history as by the collective historical context of which we are a part.

Surrender is not only joyful; it is also frightening. It often seems as if our creative efforts are blocked by an agency or influence that ties our hands until the contest between joy and anxiety has been decided. The energy that surges up in the moment of inspiration can make us cautious. When possessed by a good idea, we are apt to ignore our limits and work ourselves to exhaustion. Yet I think the fear of exhaustion can be allayed by remembering that we have much more energy than we usually assume.

The feeling of being moved by inspiration is qualitatively different from the feeling produced by the grandiose self. The grandiose self would say, "I have hold of something; I need only to grab it and I can have it all." Inspiration, on the other hand, would say: "Something has hold of me that I can only describe. When I pick it up, I receive the power to act and give shape." Without inspiration, the therapeutic attempt to help individuals become more creative would be futile.

The Jungian method for achieving the goal of personal creativity is to open the doors of consciousness to the contents of the unconscious as ideas and images rather than as disturbances. This method, called active imagination, is easier to state in theory than to carry out in practice, for it requires that the ego be stabilized to the point where these ideas can be endured. There are individual strategies for reaching this end, which can also be reached by means of an analytical relationship that is strong enough to contain whatever erupts from the depths.

Active imagination, a method for animating the unconscious, is one way to make people more creative and to give inspiration a form that will minimize the anxiety associated with the creative process. Here I am not speaking of artistic creativity, of persons who have an idea, wrestle for several years to give it form, fail in their attempt, become depressed, and contemplate suicide. I am speaking of a moderate form of creativity, which gives a boost to life without transporting us to the final brink of ecstasy and death.

Inspiration could be defined as a state of being seized and moved by thoughts, insights, ideas, and emotions that are alogical if not supralogical. In the history of the human spirit, inspiration has typically been seen as the working of a divine essence. We also notice many references in the literature on creativity to a "spark of God," such as Koestler [1964] wrote of. Even skeptics suddenly confess that they are at a loss to explain creativity without referring to some greater power that takes possession of the human individual. In the ancient conception of ecstasy, human beings take leave of themselves to make room for the god, thereby letting the god speak and act out of them. Unlike a manic person, an ecstatic person can give up his or her post as the mouthpiece of a god. In ecstasy, we step outside ourselves. It is not that we become someone or something else, nor that we become emptied; but we make room for the god, allowing the god to speak and act out of ourselves.

Many myths revolve around this theme, one example of which appears in the story of Pentecost and the Holy Spirit from the Acts of the Apostles:

When the day of Pentecost had come, they were all together in one place. And suddenly a sound came from heaven like the rush of a mighty wind, and it filled all the house where they were sitting. And there appeared to them tongues as of fire, distributed and resting on each one of them. And they were all filled with the Holy Spirit and began to speak in other tongues, as the Spirit gave them utterance. . . .

And all were amazed and perplexed, saying to one another, . . . "What does this mean?" But others mocking said, "They are filled with new wine." But Peter, standing with the eleven, lifted up his voice and addressed them, "Men of Judea and all who dwell in Jerusalem, let this be known to you, and give ear to my words. For these men are not drunk, as you suppose, since it is only the third hour of the day; but this is what was spoken by the prophet Joel:

> 'And in the last days it shall be, God declares,
> that I will pour out my Spirit upon all flesh,
> and your sons and your daughters shall prophesy,
> and your young men shall see visions,
> and your old men shall dream dreams. . .
> And I will show wonders in the heaven above
> and signs on the earth beneath,
> blood, and fire, and vapor of smoke. . . .'

(Acts 2:1–19, RSV)

It is typical that the image of fire occurs in this story of inspiration and ecstasy. Joy is associated with warmth, enthusiasm with fire, and inspiration with blazing fire. There are a number of texts in which mystical rapture can be described with the formula "Glowing is more than knowing."

Intoxication is another mystical word, if we distinguish between ordinary and extraordinary intoxication. Drunkenness from alcohol is a decadent imitation of drunkenness from beauty. In the background of alcoholism is a longing for inspiration; what is missing is the judgment to know how much is enough.

It is similar with joy: There is a point when one must stop getting inspired, otherwise one just gets drunk.

Our text says that the gift of prophecy emerged from this event of divine inspiration. Inspiration is more than a momentary existential feeling; it also involves an understanding of life that goes beyond the present moment. Inspiration involves visions, stories of the future or of the whole that awaken fervor. It may be that our era is lacking in visions and utopias because we do not take the risk that visions entail, living instead in silence as prisoners of the dimension of breadth and strangers to that of height. The story of Pentecost includes the prediction that old people will experience inspiration in the form of dreams.

The pouring out of the Holy Spirit resulted in the founding of the first Christian communities. When ecstasy fails to find rootedness in a structure, we become high-flown, as in the "high" produced by drugs outside a ritual setting. Emotion and inspiration are not enough; they must be converted into a social utopia and an interpersonal practice so that height and breadth are correlated. But the history of institutional religion is a history of increasing domination by the dimension of breadth over that of height. Inspiration, once a living experience of the spirit, evolved into a structure and an administration. Once an idea is set in stone, the original living spirit vanishes, leaving only control in its wake. Then a longing emerges for a renewing spiritual event. If you listen to the radio at Pentecost, you will hear a number of preachers who plead for a return of the living spirit and who pledge an end to control, structure, and hierarchy.

The boundaries between enthusiasm, intoxication, and ecstasy are fluid. In a state of enthusiasm, we are not yet outside ourselves; our ego boundaries are still more or less defined. In states of ecstasy or intoxication, we do go outside ourselves; our ego boundaries dissolve, and the controlling function of normal consciousness disappears. This is why the social context of ecstasy, or its reception in ritual, is so important. When the boundaries of the ego dissolve, a ritual or a human network can hold us. And when we are held together by a ritual, we can let go and give ourselves over more completely to the powers of inspiration.

Since we seldom enact these rituals today in the context of religion, ecstasy tends to be privatized, for example in drug addiction, where it can become deadly in the truest sense of the word. Ecstasy is a matter not only of heightened life, but also of death. Inspiration can turn into possession, and even creativity can degenerate into fanaticism.

Let me conclude my treatment of the subject of inspiration by suggesting that you write a reconstructed biography of inspiration. This is a difficult task, which is made easier if the longing for inspiration is taken as a signpost: When in my life did I long for inspiration? When was I especially bored? The absence of inspiration is often perceived as boredom. When was I really upset with someone because he or she failed to inspire me? When we are in love, we are inspired and feel ecstatically alive; but love also brings us the greatest disappointments when exhaustion, staleness, and criticism empty a relationship of inspiration. As you attempt to reconstruct your biography of inspiration, examine your longing for inspiration and your anger over its absence.

12.

Dionysus and Symbiosis

IN DIONYSUS we can see the symbolic expression of a cluster of emotions including inspiration, intoxication, and ecstasy, on the verge of becoming hope. Having journeyed from the existential feeling of mania and cyclothymia to heightened drive, flight of ideas, and vision, we now approach the farthest reaches of the realm of elation, where our longings take the form of frenzy, madness, and enthusiasm. Dionysus, like Wotan, is a god of inspiration and poetry.

As I was working with Dionysus, I suddenly realized that I was much more interested in what Dionysus did to those who wrote about him than I was in Dionysus himself. Karl Kerényi died before completing his last of many books on Greek mythology, *Dionysus: Archetypal Image of Indestructible Life,* leaving the task of publication to his wife. W. F. Otto's *Dionysus: Myth and Cult* envelops you with a hypnotic rhythm. There were times when I was so carried away by this rhythm that I had no idea what I had read after finishing a page. Nietzsche, in *The Birth of Tragedy,* based his thoughts on Dionysus, but he got so caught up by the spirit of Dionysus that it is difficult to tell in the end what is Dionysus and what is Nietzsche's projection onto Dionysus.

These writers criticized each other on grounds such as these. Nietzsche, it was maintained, was no longer writing about

Dionysus, but rather about the Dionysian spirit; Otto was carried away by a fantasy. I believe that Kerényi, too, was carried away by a fantasy. It seems to belong to the Dionysian spirit that persons who are basically very controlled get carried away. Kerényi collects more and more information and the picture grows increasingly complicated until he suddenly bursts into a flood of marvelous, emotional language. This is what it is like to be seized and carried away by Dionysus.

Dionysus is a symbol of "indestructible life." Let us put this expression from Karl Kerényi in the center of our inquiry. The most reliable information we have about Dionysus is probably found in Euripides' tragedy *The Bacchae*. Dionysus was a wine god, a bull god, and a god of women. Before he was a god of wine, he was a god of mead; mead, made from honey, was an intoxicating drink older than wine. But let us call him a god of wine. The feeling of a Dionysian state was described by Otto as filled with wine, possessing the strength of a bull, surrounded by worshiping women, and having no fear of snakes.

We, too, have preconceptions about what belongs to the Dionysian spirit. For most of us, the Dionysian is intoxicating, ecstatic, and strongly related to sexuality and fertility. These associations obscure many aspects of Dionysus.

When we bring together everything that has been seen in Dionysus, we have a very complex god. His first duty is to bewitch and to bring joy. He brings wine to free us from grief and sorrow. A dancer and an ecstatic lover, he liberates and heals.

The god most full of delight was at the same time the one most full of terror. Ripping apart animals, not to mention human beings, and eating their raw flesh, Dionysus was a beast of prey. He embodied a tremendous ambivalence as the bringer of both joy and destruction, and was celebrated either with great noise or with deathly silence. He was not only a god of vegetation, concerned with life on earth; he was also a god of the underworld and of death, at times equated with Hades. Heraclitus commented on a procession in which the Greeks carried a phallus: "If it were not Dionysus for whom they held their processions and sang their songs, it would have been a completely shameful act to the reverent." [Heraclitus, frag. 15, in Otto, 1981, p. 116]. The phallic symbol of fertility, crowned and paraded about, belonged to the cult of Dionysus.

Dionysus was regarded, among other things, as a divine child. This is important for us if we are to look at emotions in terms of archetypal images. The divine child represents the archetypal foundation of a child's capacity for joy. But Dionysus himself is more than a divine child.

According to one of many birth legends, Dionysus was born out of Zeus's thigh. Zeus had an affair with Semele, a mortal woman. Hera, Zeus's jealous wife, disguised herself and visited Semele, advising her to demand of Zeus that he show himself in all his splendor. Zeus could not refuse Semele's request, and she was burned to ashes by this god of lightning. Zeus quickly removed his son Dionysus from the fire and sewed him into his thigh until he was ready to be born a second time. When Dionysus came to term, Zeus bore him out of his thigh. Feminists say, "This is how the father god appropriates birth." More mythological thinkers speak of a twofold birth of the divine child, a recurrent event in mythology: birth first from a human being and then from a god.

In another version, Dionysus was the son of Persephone and Hades. Ancient Greek art often depicted him as surrounded by a number of women. Dionysus was a god of women. He had a very close relationship with his mother, with Semele or Persephone, with Demeter, and perhaps with the greatest goddess, Cybele, as well. The idea is always the same, as is repeatedly expressed in Euripides' *Bacchae:* The women around Dionysus are devotees of Cybele, the great goddess, who is responsible for both the earth and the underworld.

The divine child, Dionysus, was often depicted as a ram. The ram in Dionysus' symbolism stands for overabundant, vital life and refers also to Pan and thus to sexuality and panic. Rather than being sacrificed in the Dionysian rites, rams were to be played with.

Dionysus was also depicted on a cart drawn by panthers, riding toward Ariadne, his wife. In contrast to the other gods and goddesses, Ariadne had a constant love relationship with Dionysus, in spite of the fact that he was such an ecstatic god. It is very often stated in the literature that the panther cart has to do with Dionysus' rending, tearing nature as a beast of prey, but I do not agree. Cybele was also depicted on a panther cart, and I believe that Dionysus' close relationship with her and with the feminine included his ability to behave like a wildcat.

In other renderings from around the seventh or eighth century before Christ, Dionysus was portrayed as a divine child surrounded by wine. Much later, numerous portrayals of Christ borrowed from this iconography. Being surrounded by wine points to the wine-like nature of the child; this was understood with reference not only to its alcoholic character, but also to its origins in the grapevine, which looks like dry wood in the winter but sprouts its tendrils in the spring. This symbolizes the coincidence of death and fertility. Dionysus appears and vanishes. Not subject to any kind of control, he was often worshiped as an absent god.

Various fertility festivals held in his honor included a procession with a phallus icon. Dionysus was clearly a god of vegetation, with the symbols of ivy, the pine cone, and the grapevine. And he was a god of animals: bull, panther, and ram. The most important of Dionysus' festivals was the Anthesteria celebrated in February–March, which lasted three days. On the first day, Dionysus was invoked by singing the dithyramb. This was a ritual song and dance in which women gathered in a circle, clapped their hands, and invoked Dionysus. Stories were told, and it is out of the dithyramb that the dramatic arts were born. Here was the birth of tragedy, hence Nietzsche's book about Dionysus bearing this title.

The purpose of the ritual dithyramb was to promote ecstasy, produced by the beating of drums, dancing, and the imbibing of an intoxicating drink. The ritual dancers comprised what was called the dithyrambic choir; they were transformed and unconscious, having lost their individual identity, singing their visions in the choir. The members of the choir of Apollo, by contrast, did not lose their identity.

Dionysus was more than a god of wine, though, since wine contained within it visionary possibilities. The gift of prophecy had never been foreign to the Greek goddesses. During the Dionysian celebration, visions were formulated in words and then performed as a tragedy. Thus the gift of prophecy was very close to the art of poetry. Having invoked the god and imbibed the wine that Dionysus gave to heighten ecstasy, the gift of vision was granted, along with the capacity to formulate what was seen in the visionary state. Descriptions of this celebration reveal that the visionary state was entered into by undertaking the following activities: (1) the drinking of wine; (2) joining hands to create a mystic circle, a vessel capable of receiving divine inspiration; and (3) luring and invoking Dionysus. I am not sure that we would be so comfortable calling on the god in this manner; perhaps we would like to, but do not dare.

The god's arrival, still belonging to the first day of the celebration, was symbolized by a ship; Dionysus always came from the depths of the ocean or from the underworld. His ship was entwined with the grapevine, which sprang up from out of the depths. Dionysus' ship was an icon that depicted various aspects of his myth and cult.

One vase shows him riding in his ship, carrying his staff, accompanied by a silenus and by women. A silenus stood upright with the thighs of a horse, the torso of a man, and a huge phallus. When they grew old, sileni were sometimes called satyrs. But satyrs, unlike sileni, usually had very large bellies, which they had acquired from the consumption of wine. I believe that quite different cultural influences contributed to the image of these plump gods. In any case, they were often pictured as Dionysus' lustful companions.

Dionysus was often portrayed on a ship cart as well, a subject that has aroused a great deal of controversy. In the ship cart one typically sees the grapevine and satyrs or sileni playing flutes. There are many fairy tales in which the motif of the ship cart appears, a motif that brings with it the question, where did this ship come from? It represents the appearance of Dionysus no longer as a child but as an adult.

Dionysus' ship was at times a basket, the bow of which was the head of a mule. The mule belonged to Dionysus' symbolism less on account of its stubbornness than of its sexuality. Maenads, companions of Dionysus, also rode on mules. "Maenad" comes from the Greek word *mania,* meaning possession or frenzy. Sometimes a bull was sacrificed in the place of a mule, to the accompaniment of sacred songs.

The entire first day of Dionysus' festival is depicted on one vase: The god was invoked and arrived, a bull was sacrificed. The sacrifice provided a way of entering into the bull's strength, and it symbolized the fate of Dionysus' devotees during the festival.

On the second day, Dionysus was married to the city. Dionysus demanded absolute primacy. Dionysian emotions, deeply anchored in the body, are powerful expressions of our longings, and they too demand absolute primacy. On the third day, the souls of the dead returned, and the prayer for the dead was recited. Everything that was dead in life, and everything that one wished were dead, returned to visit the living; all that was repressed and gone now reappeared.

This festival can be thought of as a vegetation ceremony in which nature, continually dying and rising, depicts the fate of the human being. By identifying with the god, human beings are assured of continual rebirth; but they will also continually experience barrenness. This return of the repressed also represents the psychic experiences of the individual: We cannot stimulate the unconscious or allow it to flood the gates of the ego without allowing the free entry of our problems as well. We are wary of ecstasy because we know that huge portions of what we have repressed can emerge in its wake.

Very few facts have been definitively established regarding the cult of Dionysus. One reads again and again that there was frenzy and ecstasy, as is clearly depicted in *The Bacchae* of Euripides, but the exact content of Dionysian rites was kept a mystery. We know that it was a mystery for women, which must have had extremely radical social implications. Euripides described how Dionysus arrived, either noisily or in deathly silence— noisily for those who took delight in his arrival, or in deathly silence for those who were afraid. Women left their households, children, and husbands, went off into the mountains at night, danced to the sound of flutes and drums, became ecstatic from wild dancing, and were transported so far that they were sometimes discovered days later practically dead from exhaustion on the far side of Mount Parnassus. There they would lie down, their deep sleep guarded by a ring of women from the nearby village.

The outstanding features of this description of Dionysus'

cult are the trance states and the vigorous dancing movements. Then there are the various attributes of these women, who were dressed in deerskins, crowned with ivy, and girdled with snakes; they carried in their hands the so-called thyrsos, a wand wrapped in grape leaves and topped with a pine cone. These devotees were so active that they could apparently dance on stone and snow. Kerényi never tired of pointing out that women danced in the snow on Mount Parnassus at an elevation of seventy-two hundred feet during February and March.

The unbelievable aspect of the cult was that women simply left their families. It is thus not surprising that Dionysus faced a great deal of opposition. One must imagine the god arriving, the women leaving their families — men, children, and infants alike — disappearing into the forests, and dancing together. Any man who intruded was killed. The maenads not only danced; they suckled fawns and the cubs of wild wolves and tore and ate raw meat with their bare hands.

The goat, a victim of sacrifice to Dionysus, probably functioned as a scapegoat. It has been observed that the goat's blood was necessary to fructify the barren March grapevine. The treatment of the goat was analogous to the treatment of Dionysus, who was killed repeatedly. Symbolic death and killing are features of ecstatic experience as well: Ecstasy carries us beyond our limits, killing our normal personality. It can fragment us so that we do not know how — or if — we are going to return.

A scapegoat must be punished with death because of the sins attached to it. But why should a goat be a sinful animal? This equation is conceivable only when the sins we are capable of committing are projected on to the goat. Dionysus attracts many of our projections about sexuality as sin. I do not believe that this is the most sinful aspect of Dionysian-inspired behavior, though. Breaking out of the social order is a much more dangerous aspect, which causes us to approach inspiration and ecstasy with caution.

Dionysus was also a god of masks. He had two masks, one made out of fig wood, depicting him as an old man, and the other made out of grapevine, depicting him as a young bridegroom. When the god was absent, he was dwelling in one of his masks. Dionysus was invoked by putting on the mask. These mask celebrations, like Mardi Gras practices, were based on belief in transformation and on riotous frenzy. The basic theme of Dionysian religion was transformation not only through spiritualization but also through wild frenzy and bodily rapture.

The mysteries of Dionysus provided a ritual means of participating in the godhead. The definition of ecstasy as the possession of a human being by a god is perfectly appropriate here. There was then a great deal of physical strength and invulnerability attributed to fire and weapons. There were miracles well before the time of Christ: Water was struck out of stones and turned into wine; rivers flowed with milk. When we look at these miracles symbolically, we perceive that the essential miracle is movement. Water transformed into wine suggests that the Dionysian state brings us to the point where we can see inspiration in the most ordinary things. To be gifted for inspiration means not only living in ecstasy but also finding inspiration in everyday life. Dionysus was a god of abundance, and ecstasy is an abundance that pulls us out of the order we have established for ourselves; this may have good or evil consequences.

The Dionysian mysteries were for women. They were explosive mysteries, which probably filled an important need of women to make their contribution to the transition from the non-living to the living, and to be able to awaken this god of death to life. Eventually the men could no longer tolerate this situation. It is said that Athena — a manlike goddess — broke the ancient vow and let men participate in the mysteries, but they had to dress themselves in women's clothing. From then on, the vitality of the cult of Dionysus began to wane.

The question remains why this was an exclusively women's rite. Various explanations have been offered. Otto found the answer in the fact that only women can give birth and nurse. Kerényi observed that women have always been more adept as visionaries. The incredible turbulence out of which a vision came to birth was, in his view, the central feature of the Dionysian cult and an act that women have more talent for by nature. It is quite clear that natural psychic energies were set free by a cult of life that emerged from the depths, bringing a new order into being, at least for a while. These women left the established order; it seems we can never hear enough about how sinful they were.

Many stories were invented about the sileni and what an incredibly orgiastic time they had. *The Bacchae* includes a passage in which a shepherd says, "What you have said about the sileni is not true. The women lie down next to each other in the forest. There are no men among them." Perhaps this revelation is even more problematic. It shows that when the Dionysian spirit takes hold, not only do the power and vitality of ecstasy arise, but the old order is also endangered. A new order could be established, not in the usual manner of patching things up a bit by adding footnotes to the old order but in the sense of a truly visionary change.

This inherent danger is well illustrated by the fate of Pentheus in *The Bacchae,* who is dead set against Dionysus and is torn limb from limb by his own mother when he tries to visit the maenads disguised in women's clothing. Translated into psychological terms, this means that withdrawing oneself from a state of ecstasy drives one to insanity. Emotions of a Dionysian intensity demand submission. Inspiration cannot be set aside;

it must be taken up and given form. Euripides differentiated between true and false bacchantes. The true ones were truly seized, the false merely gushed with pseudoemotion. It is the same with us today.

Through their identification with the god, women devoted to Dionysus were connected to vital and cosmic powers. Their souls, experiencing something like indestructible life, became immortal and divine. These women crossed over the limits of the human condition to experience a liberation, freedom, and spontaneity that was otherwise unknown. Entering into a symbiosis with nature and expanding into the cosmos, they were no longer subject to the old rules. They evaded an order that had held them in place. Naturally this can be a decisive experience for women.

Psychologically we could say that these women were inflated. Yet their identification with higher powers did not obliterate all structure; ritual mystery provided a setting for ecstasy, although some women did take leave of their senses. We get the impression that those who fought against Dionysus were more likely to go insane than those who let Dionysus have his way with them. In any case, we could speak of a possession by or identification with transpersonal powers in which the archetype of Dionysus took the place of the ego.

The archetype of Dionysus has moved many writers, among them Kerényi, Otto, and Nietzsche. In *The Birth of Tragedy*, Nietzsche described what it is like to be seized by Dionysus:

> Dionysiac stirrings arise either through the influence of those narcotic potions of which all primitive races speak in their hymns, or through the powerful approach of Spring, which penetrates with joy the whole frame of nature. So stirred, the individual forgets himself completely. It is the same Dionysiac power which in medieval Germany drove ever increasing crowds of people singing and dancing from place

to place; we recognize in these St. John's and St. Vitus' dancers the bacchic choruses of the Greeks, who had their precursors in Asia Minor and as far back as Babylon and the orgiastic Sacaea. There are people who, either from lack of experience or out of sheer stupidity, turn away from such phenomena, and, strong in the sense of their own sanity, label them either mockingly or pityingly "endemic diseases." These benighted souls have no idea how cadaverous and ghostly their "sanity" appears as the intense throng of Dionysiac revelers sweeps past them.

Not only does the bond between man and man come to be forged once more by the magic of the Dionysiac rite, but nature itself, long alienated or subjugated, rises again to celebrate the reconciliation with her prodigal son, man. The earth offers its gifts voluntarily, and the savage beasts of mountain and desert approach in peace. The chariot of Dionysus is bedecked with flowers and garlands; panthers and tigers stride beneath his yoke. If one were to convert Beethoven's "Ode to Joy" into a painting, and refuse to curb the imagination when that multitude prostrates itself reverently in the dust, one might form some apprehension of Dionysiac ritual. Now the slave emerges as a freeman; all the rigid, hostile walls which either necessity or despotism has erected between men are shattered. Now that the gospel of universal harmony is sounded, each individual becomes not only reconciled to his fellow, but actually at one with him—as though the veil of Maya had been torn apart and there remained only shreds floating before the vision of mystical Oneness. Man now expresses himself through song and dance as the member of a higher community; he has forgotten how to walk, how to speak, and is on the brink of taking wing as he dances. Each of his gestures betokens enchantment. . . .

According to Nietzsche, possession by Dionysus heightens the bond between persons, removes boundaries, and effaces class differences. Competition comes to a halt, and individuals are torn out of their isolation. The historian of religion Mircea Eliade likewise noted that Dionysus effaced social differences, speaking alike to farmers, politicians, intellectuals, contemplatives, partakers in orgies, and ascetics. And the Hellenistic philosopher Plotinus spoke of ecstasy as the exit from individuality into an intoxicating fusion. Not only do individuals find accord with each other, but human beings find accord with nature as well.

As humanity and nature blend harmoniously together, the question whether nature rules humanity or humanity rules nature is rendered irrelevant. Rediscovering an original unity, the entire creation converges in an *unus mundus,* to use Jung's term [Jung, 1955–56]. As Nietzsche expressed it, "The mystical jubilation of Dionysus . . . breaks the spell of individuation and opens a path to the maternal womb of being" [p. 97]. This oneness is no deception and no drunken illusion, but rather the revelation of a deeper human reality in which the instant becomes eternity, so that space and time are altered to create complete openness to the future.

In Jungian psychology this means the coincidence of the self with the suprapersonal Self or *unus mundus.* In Indian mythology it would be expressed as a meaningful coincidence of the personal Atman with the transpersonal Atman.

But Dionysus is not only sought after; he is also fled from. Fusion and dissolution into a greater wholeness, effecting a loss of individuation, produce anxiety and defensiveness as well. In *The Bacchae,* Pentheus went mad after struggling against Dionysus.

Dionysus' counterpart is Apollo. Deifying the principle of individuation, Apollo stands for measure and the maintenance of individual boundaries. Apollo was an ethical god who symbolized the values of balance and self-knowledge, although he was also a god of prophecy, the arts, music, and archery. Apollo brought the evil in the world under control, and he was responsible for peace, respect for the law, and divine harmony. But he was not free of vengefulness, jealousy, or deceit. The Dionysian spirit, in contrast to the ethical spirit of Apollo, seems titanic and barbaric. But we must not forget that the oracle of Delphi, the property of Apollo, was guarded by Dionysus during the winter when Apollo was away. In the summer Apollo returned.

Apollo inspired visions, insight, meditation, wisdom, and music. But his inspiration was a step removed from the immediateness and weight of life. His calmness and serenity implied mental concentration. The famous Delphic oracle "Know Thyself!" lacked a wild immediacy. There was ecstasy mediated by a god, but no ecstasy in fellowship with a god. Nietzsche felt that the opposition between Apollo and Dionysus was necessary, each spurring the other on, and he maintained that Apollo could only be understood against the Dionysian background. Nietzsche prescribed a formula for human balance that is reminiscent of Binswanger's: Only as much of the Dionysian spirit should enter into consciousness as can be appropriated by the Apollonian power of clarification.

Another form of ecstasy, such as we find in the mysticism of Teresa of Avila, is an undifferentiated unity with the All. It might be expressed: "I am in You; You are in me." In this formless experience, the ego is dissolved in an absolute You. The Dionysian form of ecstasy, by contrast, would be expressed, "I am taken hold of, seized, possessed, made part of a whole, lost." The possibility of losing the ego and self in ecstasy creates a fear of ecstasy, a fear that we experience in a milder form with sexuality. We often hear of persons who keep themselves under control during the sexual act and then complain that no ecstasy is possible for them. Since their ego structure is endangered by the unconscious, they are afraid that they will lose themselves if they become orgasmic and ecstatic.

This is also the reason why the biography of joy should be written before biographies of inspiration and ecstasy; the ego must be stabilized before it is ready to absorb large concentrations of inspiration. It may be enough to use the *longing* for inspiration and ecstasy as signposts guiding us into this realm. An unconscious longing for ecstatic visions may well be a characteristic of our age. We should at least permit ourselves these longings, even if we are no longer so open to ecstasy itself.

To be taken hold of by Dionysus means to be possessed, and to permit oneself to be possessed. It signifies entry into a symbiosis rather than individuation. We often hear that mystics are able to establish a symbiosis with the divine without ceasing to individuate, having found a good rhythm between symbiosis and individuation. This balance can be explained psychologically by the fact that the more defined the ego boundaries are, the greater their permeability is.

Issues of symbiosis and individuation are typical of but not restricted to a phase in early childhood development. They form a theme encountered throughout the human life span. We know that symbiosis in early childhood lays a strong foundation for healing later in life. Therapists are attempting to make it possible for their patients to reexperience these healing powers. Hapnotherapy, a recently founded type of therapy, employs bodily touching with the goal of reactivating the original mother-child symbiosis, reaching back in some cases as far as the prenatal symbiosis, in order to liberate healing energies and new powers of resistance.

Viewing this therapeutic strategy from the perspective of the archetype of Dionysus, we would say that elated moods offer a holding environment that promotes symbiosis and expansion into the world. The ecstasy of symbiosis is the best pre-condition for both solidarity and expansion into the cosmos, but we must never forget to step back into reality again.

Nietzsche distinguished between the Greek Dionysiacs and the barbarian Dionysiacs, who were merely boisterous and cruel. Does Dionysus play a role in today's world apart from the drinking bouts and sex orgies that lose themselves in the riots of the barbarian Dionysus?

Dionysus has gripped everyone who has written about him with hope in the indestructibility of life. Dionysus bewitches modern dreams as well. We would not expect him to appear in his Greek costume, but rather in the form of image clusters that have a Dionysian effect. As an example, let me quote the dream of a thirty-nine-year-old woman.

> A group of women join together in a large circle in the mid-dle of a meadow. A ritual should begin. I feel the drums throbbing in my body. The circle remains open in one place, which upsets me; don't these people know that this hole disrupts everything? Then I find myself in a bar, talking an-grily about how these people have no sense for ecstasy. I talk myself into a rage and gulp down a glass of wine. I am so upset, I am practically going out of my mind. I speak to a foreign-looking man with long, curly hair and radiant eyes. As I speak, I find myself dancing. Next to him is a man who looks a little like the Devil (horns, billy-goat beard, satyric). I feel an incredible surge of power. Now I can close the cir-cle. The man says, "The opening in the circle was for me and my ship." I think he must be drunk. I wake up very stimulated and alive. I feel like breaking out of everything that has held me back until now. I don't understand why I am always so careful and dependent on what others think of me. I have an incredible desire to turn everything upside down.

This woman had certainly heard of Dionysus, but she did not know that the ancient Dionysus normally arrived in a ship; she thought that the man in her dream must be drunk when he spoke of his ship. There are several image clusters in this dream that combine to produce a Dionysian effect. The group of women forming a large circle would represent the invocation of Dionysus (or possibly of some other male divinity or animus spirit), including drumming and dancing. Now comes the first obstacle: The circle is not closed. The personal chain is broken. Here the dream comes closer to reality. The dreamer goes into a bar, lectures about ecstasy, is furious, talks herself into a rage, drinks wine, is so upset that she could go out of her mind. The Dionysian spirit already has her fully in its grip. In Jungian terms, the foreign-looking man would represent an animus figure: a fascinating, foreign man with long, curly hair, and glowing eyes. The dance returns again. The association of Dionysus with the devil is supported historically by the fact that Dionysus was often seen as the Devil in Christian eyes. I believe that the most crucial aspect of the dream is the effect it has on the dreamer: Like the maenads, this woman had the feeling she could leave behind all the structures that were holding her back, in order to let something really new into her life.

The myths of Dionysus bring into consciousness those images and psychic processes which belong to the cluster of emotions that includes enthusiasm, inspiration, intoxication, and ecstasy. Thus it brings us to the outermost pole of the elated emotions. If we allow these mythic images to play on our imaginations, the corresponding emotions will also be touched in our psyches. Meanwhile it is becoming clearer that all these emotions are based on the emotion of hope, which keeps shining through in such forms as Dionysus, the symbol of indestructible life.

PART V

Hope

13.

Sisyphus's Hidden Hope

HOPE IS THE EMOTION on which all the other emotions of elation are grounded. But it is a relatively abstract emotion, which
is why I have approached it from the perspective of joy and inspiration. I prefer not to write about hope alone, but rather
about the whole range of emotions that includes expectation
and longing.

We have seen that there is a harmony in the present moment of joy when we not only feel in tune with ourselves and
the world as it is, but when we also have the sense that the
moment can only expand. There is a feeling of promise, as if
we were in store for a pleasant surprise. The present moment
of joy contains the seed of the future. In expectation and hope,
the future blooms to occupy a central place.

We can form a more concrete idea of hope if we think about
what it is like to be without hope. Longing is much easier to
describe: Longing is like stretching into the distance in a desperate attempt to come closer to the object of our desire. Hope
is a much less conspicuous feeling, though no less important.
We speak of hope in terms of a turn for the better, in the near
or distant future, the final shape of which is still unknown.
The change may be just around the bend, or it may come only
in the next world. We speak of hope when our lives become
shaped by a glimpse of something not yet clearly within sight.

Hope draws its persuasive power from a vision yet to be unveiled. Inspiration ensues when the vision is revealed. Since hope's authority derives from a vision that is still shrouded, it is risky to try to penetrate the vision; we can only sense what lies within. It is as if we turn toward a light that does not yet exist, though we have the impression that it must. The darkest hour is just before dawn, we say to ourselves.

Hope is the emotion that relates us to the future. Another emotion that relates us to the future is anxiety. The prospect of the future can fill us with anxiety or with hope. Hope, the opposite of anxiety, offers consolation. When I say I can hope again, I mean I am consoled with the sense of something better somewhere in the future. Hope can drive us onward, but hope's main characteristic is that it affords us a feeling of safety and security. Hope does not impel us the way inspiration or ecstasy does; it allows us to find shelter in life. We must not forget that hope includes the unhoped for, a dialectic to be taken seriously. In hope we long for what we had never expected, as if we were trusting in the future in spite of knowing better. Hope is not reasonable; it is the unseen vision, and prone to taking risks. Hope always looks toward creative changes — by definition, changes for the better.

There are various ways to interpret hope. From the perspective of Lersch [1970], we can maintain that it is impossible to exist without any hope at all; hope, an expression of the will to live, can never be fully absent from life. According to this definition, it is not possible not to hope. Henseler argues that someone who commits suicide does so out of the hope that death will be better than life. Not even death can separate us from this hope for something better; we can deny it, but we cannot banish it from life. This view is supported by the experience of persons who are going through difficult times but say, "Something in me just keeps on living. I know it will get better sometime." Even terminally ill persons express the feeling that things will somehow get better. And those without any conception of a life after death — who say, "I am sure that when I die, that is the end of it" — still maintain that "It's getting better" or, at least, "I hope it will get better." This is a sign that as long as we live, we live for a better future.

From the perspective of depth psychology, hope can be seen as an expression of an individual's trust in life. Someone who has a solid foundation of basic trust (to use Erikson's term [1959], which has become a convention in the literature) to draw on from early childhood will have more hope, and deficient basic trust diminishes possibilities for hope. Hope is bound up with our parental complexes, and the depth of our hope correlates with the extent to which these parental complexes are sustaining. This is one explanation of hope; no explanation is exhaustive. Hope seems too fundamental to receive any final explanation, although many attempts have been made to discover its hidden background.

To enlarge on the depth psychological theory of basic trust, we can draw on another explanation of hope: We each have a vision of our lives, a vision of our wholeness that is still unconscious. Since we know somewhere within us where we are going, we have ground for hope. The idea that the unconscious is ahead of us is expressed in the Jungian definition of the Self: the Self comprises the personality in the past, the present, and the future. The entire process of individuation is present in the unconscious and can make itself known in the form of a vision.

More religiously motivated thinkers such as Gabriel Marcel [1964] maintain that hope is a grace, a gift. Less religiously oriented thinkers such as Ernst Bloch say that hope can be learned. Bloch's book *Das Prinzip Hoffnung* (The Principle of Hope) has influenced me greatly. In a very interesting preface, he wrote, "Hope extinguishes anxiety; learning to hope is what counts."

Bloch strongly opposes our tendency to learn fear. He believes that we should set out to learn hope. It is very provocative to assert that hope can be learned, and even more provocative to claim to teach hope.

According to another, very different view, hope is a way of evading life, an illusion rather than a hidden guide or vision of the future. Thus people are always foolish enough to imagine that things are getting better, even though they know it is not so. Therapists are quick to react against this view because even if we are in a very bad situation but have preserved at least the vision of something better, we are not yet completely lost. The question whether hope is a vision of what can be, or simply an illusion, is a serious philosophical and psychological issue.

We can sort out what has been written about hope by distinguishing between these two basic perspectives. The first maintains that without hope one cannot live, since hope represents the human being's basic source of *Geborgenheit* (safety, security, protectedness) upon which all higher feelings—and the energy for action—nourish themselves. The other perspective argues that hope is the easy way out, and that living in constant hope of something better jeopardizes and devalues the here and now of our actual lives. When we are busy hoping for something else, the joy of everyday life slips away from us.

I question whether it is really hope that destroys our enjoyment of the present. Allow me to quote a few sentences from Bloch in which he deals with the opposition between hope as our most basic sense of *Geborgenheit* and as the "easy way out."

> What matters is learning to hope. Hope does not abandon its post. It is in love with success rather than failure. Hope, superior to fear, is neither passive like its inferior nor imprisoned in nothingness. Hope reaches out; it broadens rather than narrows. This affect summons persons who actively throw themselves into the process of becoming, to which

they belong. It does not tolerate the life of a dog that allows itself to be passively flung into the would-be, the inscrutable, and the grudgingly accepted. How richly has every era dreamed, dreamed of a better life that was possible. The lives of all people are filled with daydreams, many of which are merely vapid, an enervating escape, booty for swindlers. But within these daydreams there is also something that opens our eyes, prevents us from being satisfied with mere leftovers, and outlaws abdication. This has hope at its core and can be taught. [Block, 1959, p. 1]

Bloch saw hope in daydreaming, fantasy, and imagination. Through fantasy and imagination, we draw the future into the present. He concedes that this can be a mere daydream, a form of escapism, but he insists that it can also move us to improve our lot. For things to get better, we have to see more than their present state. Imagination is the way we expand our vision. According to Bloch, we cannot know whether our imagination is an escape or the seed of a new truth and new activity. And yet I believe that we can readily discern the difference within ourselves; if a fantasy does not engage the will but only calms us, then I would suspect it of being an escape. Those who are always suspicious of imagination are often heavily influenced by existentialist thought. Besides, we have the right to escape now and then.

The idea that hope is an escape, a way of evading life, is very prominent in French existentialism, especially as expressed by Camus in *The Myth of Sisyphus*, which appeared in 1942. French existentialism must also be seen as a product of its time. "The typical act of avoidance, the fatal evasion, that is . . . hope," Camus wrote. "Hope of another life one must 'deserve'" is a fatal evasion, "or deception of those who live not for life itself but for some great idea that will transcend it, refine it, give it a meaning, and betray it." I am interested now not in whether Camus was right or wrong, but rather in the influence that his trend of thought exercised, leading to a steady stream of books in the 1950s about hope (including those of Bloch and Bollnow).

Camus's extremely one-sided position demanded a response. Soon after Camus's statement about hope as a fatal evasion appeared, Gabriel Marcel, also in Paris, published a philosophy of hope with the message that no one can live without hope.

Camus's maxim was that life must be lived here and now, regardless of approval or disapproval, not in the next world with an eye to a home in heaven. Life wants to be lived actively, affirmatively, immediately. What does this mean more specifically? "It is evident when a person takes on challenges that present themselves and does not turn away from anything — neither from the world nor from our absurd situation as human beings." Camus viewed human beings as absurd heroes. This implied that we must recognize the extent of our wretched state. Facing the world is a challenge on the one hand, and a call to consciousness on the other.

The symbolic hero embodying this philosophy was Sisyphus, hence *The Myth of Sisyphus*. Camus used only the second part of the Greek myth, in which Sisyphus pushes a stone up a hill without any prospect of success; the stone, shortly before reaching the top, rolls back down into the valley. Sisyphus goes as far as he can before the stone rolls down again of its own weight, pushing the stone back up again with the utmost exertion. Camus reflected that Sisyphus has no prospect of success, but he is not desperate either. Thus Sisyphus depotentiates the gods who have punished him. Camus's basic message could be stated as follows: When we actively affirm our fate in simple obedience to whatever presents itself at the moment, life has meaning after all. Camus concludes with the exciting sentence, "The struggle itself toward the heights is enough to fill a human heart; we must imagine Sisyphus as a happy man."

Jean Paul Sartre (for example, in *L'existentialisme est un humanisme*) held that what counts in life is absolute engagement. One cannot expect to be rewarded or count on things improving. Both Sartre and Camus argued against hope and for absolute engagement. But Sartre would never demand that an absurd hero be happy. It was Camus's novel suggestion that not only does the human condition require toleration of failure, but furthermore we should be happy with this lot. However, I question whether hope does not find a way into this philosophy through the back door, through happiness. Sisyphus has a future. He must expect the gods eventually to lose their nerve in the face of his Stoic resolve.

Camus fought against decadent forms of hope. I am of the opinion that he did not finally oppose hope itself; what he opposed could better be described as expectation. We have two ways of using the word hope: "I hope" and "I hope that. . . ." When we say "I hope that . . ." we often become quite nebulous. We hope that something will change for the better. But we do not necessarily hope with all our heart and soul. We just want. Camus fights against this: Rather than entertaining some nebulous hope, let us be alert and acknowledge what the precise problem is. This can be a very healthy attitude. It forces us to deal with problems here and now, to take responsibility for matters that require attention, to stand with both feet planted firmly on the ground.

Camus also opposed delegation, arguing that "my stone is my problem. My fate is my problem." For example, he opposed the attitude that says, "I've just had bad luck. If my father, if my mother, if the government, if the environment. . . ." Camus battled against the delegation of responsibility, against denial and projection. When we own our problems and answer for them ourselves, the result is maximal freedom to create our own world. There is no one to tell us what is finally right and true. We must live on the side of risk and make the best of it.

This philosophy is insufficient. Sisyphus is incomplete, especially if we consider only the second part of his myth [see Kast, 1986]. Sisyphus is a solitary, proud, perhaps even autistic hero. He is completely by himself. And he is a hero who acts as if consciousness were primary: "I can do what I want. No one has to help me." There is no one else inhabiting the Sisyphusian landscape. Sisyphus is not a narcissistic hero; there is no audience—not even himself—to applaud as he sets his face to his stone. He is a solitary hero. The principle of relationship is completely absent in this existentialist strand of thought. There is no relationship, for that would mean the risk of getting into something that one might not be able to live up to. And there is nothing that simply comes one's way. One must work hard for everything. I believe there are times when we have to work hard for everything, but there are also times when something just comes our way. Sisyphus is a paramount hero of the ego. You see, Camus deposes all authorities and puts the ego in the seat of authority.

I have yet to meet anyone who has not at some time in life been influenced by French existentialism. The battle against foggy hope has a place in nearly everyone's life, above all when the ego complex must develop out of the parental complexes and when our lives call for greater autonomy. Autonomy, not autism. In other words, at times when a person feels threatened by authority complexes, Camus's teaching can help him or her to say, "No one is going to get me out of what I have gotten myself into. Later I will have to pay for it all. So I am going to do as I please." Revolt may then break out in a person's life, which might be necessary in order to win autonomy. But autonomy can easily become isolationism, taking us away from relationships and from the ground that supports us.

In my opinion, this existentialism developed in an atmosphere of hostility to depth psychology. There was a time when depth psychology would say more emphatically, "Just go along with it! Regress! Wait until something happens!" Do you know how long one can wait in obedience to this attitude? Nothing happens! I can understand how persons without much patience might say, "For heaven's sake, now we need to emphasize the here and now!" This happened in depth psychology, too. "Here and now" was practically the prayer of the sixties and seventies. But that refrain has subsided again somewhat. "Here and now" is simply no longer enough, because there is no future in it.

French existentialism unleashed an intense reaction with such books as *About Hope* [Plügge, 1954] and the following sentence from Bollnow: "It is not just a matter of discovering hope; it is a matter of finding new sources of *Geborgenheit*. To demobilize hope would be to demobilize *Geborgenheit*" [1955, p. 12]. French existentialism is an antidote to regression and the tendency to obscure. It does not speak for every aspect of life. Mythology consists of more mythologems than Sisyphus. If Sisyphus were the only hero, his task would be our task. But he is not.

When we call hope an illusion, we are saying more about expectation than about hope. Both expectation and hope lead us into the future. Possessing a specific content, expectation is more definite than hope. We *hope* that something will get better, sensing that something — undefined — will develop. An expectation is clearer and more limited than hope.

We dealt briefly with expectation and longing earlier, when we were discussing the anticipation of joy. The anticipation of joy involves a significant degree of risk, the risk of disappointment, since the joy before is not restricted to things in the present or the past but feeds on the imagination of what might happen. Imagination is informed by our knowledge of what can realistically be expected, but it is also heavily colored by our longings and wishes.

When we expect something, we live in expectation of it and our expectations structure the future. The future fills us with at least as much anxiety as hope. Everything that is so open and unstructured gives us the feeling, "My God, what do I do now?" We prepare ourselves for the future with the help of considered expectations about how things will be. If I wake up one morning and say to myself, "Today there is nothing I absolutely have to do," I will usually soon begin thinking, "What should I do now?" Expectations of what needs to be done and what I would like to do rush in to fill the vacuum. The day takes on a structure; I can keep myself busy and relieve myself of the stress of not knowing what to expect. It may be that we create general and specific expectations to structure our lives if we have no set expectations already established.

Expectations structure our lives enormously. If you have a very clear expectation—for example, a date on which you intend to take an examination—your whole life revolves around this one thought. If you live your life in the expectation of a certain encounter so that you think "Then this person will come and it will be something like this," you will not have much libido for anything else; you will be too focused on your expectation. This is why we are always so disappointed when things do not turn out the way we imagined they would. Our disappointments empty us because they announce the end of whatever was holding our psychic lives together. There is nothing else to occupy the central and now vacant position left by the old expectation until we have installed a new expectation in our lives.

Emptiness need not be as dramatic as it is always described

as being. I have come to the conclusion that the statement "I feel empty" always has a slightly unpleasant sound to the ears of therapists, as if the patient were saying, "How do I fill the emptiness again?" In terms of psychic housekeeping, emptiness signals the need for a time of restructuring, when we look to see if something new is emerging on either the inner or outer horizon.

Longings often influence our expectations. Longings express themselves mostly in the form of wishes. Whatever is animated in the unconscious, whatever must be or wants to be lived at the moment, finds expression as a wish. The intensity of our longing to have a wish fulfilled tells us how necessary the desired thing is to make us feel well and whole again. Longing has to do with living for the future. Something is always missing from our lives, and something new is continually appearing on the horizon that we can see only through the lens of our longings.

Longings easily become associated with expectations. There are not many people who can simply say, "Now I am going to tend to my longings." Longings usually flow into the molds of expectations, where they solidify. We become absorbed in thoughts about what is most important to us in life, what is in store for us, what we are looking forward to in the future. If we can achieve some distance from these fantasies, we suddenly realize how many of our longings are mixed in with them. If we manage to say, "Ah yes, those are my longings and not what I can expect from another person right now," then we can redeem the longings and avoid a huge disappointment. But since we are not usually so conscious, we generally have to be disappointed and emptied first; then perhaps we will begin to reflect.

Expectation always includes longing. The word "expectation" covers a broad spectrum of meanings. At one end of the spectrum, it involves hoping for something; this expectation is not as open-ended as a pure hope or as rigid as a definite expectation. A more definite expectation is expressed by saying, "I hope that. . . ." This can very easily slip into counting on something, or even insisting on the right to something. Expectation can be very forceful.

When we have an expectation, we are so focused on and excited about something that we seldom have a great deal of patience. Expectation is rather impatient; hope is relatively patient. Hope, unlike expectation, does not demand immediate results. Aiming at a more distant future, hope enjoys a greater freedom to let events unfold in their own time. Expectation moves in on things, whereas with hope things move in on people. Expectation is less spacious and more restricted than hope, denying receptivity to anything that does not conform to its preconceptions. Expectation makes us very choosy.

Narrowness and lack of receptivity are often due to complexes that keep surfacing in our lives. Caught in a rut, we are hardly in a position to enjoy the expansiveness of hope. To replace expectation with hope is one of the fundamental challenges of therapy. Many persons say, "I don't expect anything anymore; that way nobody can disappoint me anymore." This may be good or bad, depending on who says it. It is good if it comes from a person who has rigid expectations, someone who requires everyone else to satisfy immediate desires that are actually his or her own responsibility. It is bad if it comes from someone who no longer has any more expectations of anyone else or of life, who thus no longer wants to live.

But expectation is not confined to narrowness; it can open itself up to hope as well. It would be a mistake to try to live without any expectations at all. How would you feel if your partner said, "I don't expect anything more of you"? Such a statement drives away the future, possibilities for change, and the process of relationship as a whole. The illusion of having no expectations brings about the very thing we were trying to avoid in the first place: the threat to today. When we are fixed in the expectation of having no expectations, then the possibility truly arises that we will lose the here and now and the joy of everyday life.

I would like to conclude this chapter with a poem by Annette von Droste-Hülshoff entitled "Carpe diem" (Seize the Day), which urges us not to let empty expectations take the place of life.

> Carpe diem (Pflücke die Stunde)
> O wer nur ernst und fest die Stund ergreift
> den Kranz ihr auch von bleichen Locken streift,
> dem spendet willig sie die reichste Beute.
> Doch wir, wir Toren, drängen sie zurück,
> vor uns die Hoffnung, hinter uns das Glück
> und unsere Morgen morden unsere Heute.

> Those who seize the hour with zest and purpose,
> lifting a crown from its pale locks,
> easily reap the richest bounty.
> But we fools force it out of our way
> with hope before us, happiness behind,
> and our tomorrows murder our todays.

14.

Hope in the Realm of
the Mother Archetype

Hope draws on a hidden vision of the better. By hoping, we walk toward a light that we do not see but sense somewhere in the darkness of the future. Without hope we say, "The dark is just dark. You can imagine as many lights as you like; there are none." Hope can be understood as an open-ended orientation for the better extending as far into the future as the afterlife. This "better" is sometimes also called holy.

Hope refers to the openness of the future; as a response to the openness of the future it is an alternative to anxiety. If we are to overcome our anxiety in the face of the future, we must depend in the end on hope, but we need not take such a detour. We could react directly to the future's uncertainty by hoping, possibly even against our better judgment. We would then be drawing on creative options and resources we may never have thought we had. Hope is the emotion that works against convention and habit.

As psychologists, we are confronted with a difficult question here. We are familiar with the so-called repetition compulsion, the fact that when persons react out of their complexes they behave the same way every time. A certain quality of resignation enters psychology through this knowledge, and so we overlook the other side of the coin. It is often true that the repetition compulsion is at work, but reality may turn out differently from what theory would predict. Openness to the future is also a fact.

We have examined various theories about hope and have found one thing they all share: a careful differentiation between illusion and vision. Hope can lead to the illusion that life is other than it really is. Are we avoiding something by hoping? Is hope really a vision, the basic stuff of personal development, the raw material for the development of every person and a common life on this planet? Is hope the ground of promise that undergirds a better existential feeling, or is it a mere flight?

I have made copious use of French existentialism, which stimulated various philosophies of hope in response. Among the existentialists we witnessed a crusade against the power of illusion to deceive us into opting for spurious hope. The basic message of Camus and Sartre affirmed the value of absolute commitment, even in the absence of any prospect of success or change. In addition, Camus expected us to be happy with this state of affairs. We questioned whether this was not asking too much. It was exciting to discover a hope hidden within this philosophy, however, a hope that remains pure and imageless by rejecting all visions and constructs of happiness: Carry on even though there is no prospect of success! The feeling that it is meaningful to carry on after all reveals a hidden hope. French existentialism sought to avoid the production of false hope, battling against pipe dreams and castles in the air, against the tendency to lie in a stupor of postponed reality. I think we are all familiar with the misuse of imaginary worlds that do not deserve the name of hope. As Annette von Droste-Hülshoff wrote in the poem that I quoted, "our tomorrows murder our todays."

But there is another side to this crusade against hope. French existentialism glorified routine. This is exemplified in Sisyphus's devotion to his singular task: always the same stone. Elsewhere I have demonstrated that the stone took on a different form after having rolled down that hill so many times. There was just a bit of hope at work. I reject futile routine.

Earlier we asked if the visionary, "imaginary world" aspect of hope is really hope and not more like rigid expectation. I spoke of the cluster of emotions that includes expectation, longing, and hope, which I understand as a continuum with a very narrow, specific expectation at one end of the spectrum devoid of longing, and an expectation that increasingly resembles hope as it becomes invested with more and more longing toward the other end of the spectrum. A step outside the "visible" spectrum on the side of hope would bring us to absolute hope, to use Marcel's expression, or to universal hope as Bollnow called it, or to imageless hope as it has also been called. This form of hope is practically identical with faith, at least according to Marcel. I see expectation, longing, and hope as a continuum, with openness increasing from left to right (as it were). Absolute hope would be just off the scale. Previously we agreed that illusion has to do with narrow expectation.

Bloch speaks essentially of those expectations which are invested with longing. If we were to pose our question to Bloch about whether hope can be stimulated, he would answer unambiguously that hope can not only be learned but it can also be taught. Bloch's hope, a knowing hope rather than a spurious one, begins by being "knowingly dissatisfied" and by rejecting deficiency. I understand "knowing dissatisfaction" as a state that arises when it is clear that things could be better. Bloch further maintains that hope for as yet unborn possibilities is a normal constituent of human consciousness. To learn hope is to discover the not yet conscious. Bloch inveighs against depth psychology because he has the impression that it is not at all concerned with the future, as if the unconscious consisted of nothing but memory. While this may be true of certain currents in depth psychology, those which work with archetypal symbols deal with the anticipatory dimension of the psyche too. In the larger world the assumption is commonly made that memory is decisive, whereas anticipation is romantic and speculative. The anticipatory function is no more or less precise than the recollective function; both can be handled more or less speculatively. There is no basis here for devaluing the anticipatory function of the psyche.

Bloch was concerned with the prospective dimension of symbols, the not yet conscious that may yet become conscious. A complex is the expression of a conflict, but it is also an opportunity for development. Memory can function as a signpost guiding us into the future. The method of active imagination can help us to work out the not-yet-conscious dimension of symbols and complexes, which is not only the dimension of the future but also that of freedom. The quest to make conscious what is not yet conscious was Bloch's quest, and it is the quest of creative persons, young persons, and pilgrims in times of change. We become conscious of the not yet conscious by examining our daydreams and imaginary worlds. Indirectly Bloch was a very good psychologist, asking what distinguishes illusion from vision and offering a very succinct answer: Fantasy is illusory when it indulges us and shields us from everyday reality; it is visionary when it agitates, animates, and creates a productive tension.

Hope can be learned first by our being knowingly dissatisfied and rejecting deficiency, and then by our pursuing the daydreams and imaginary worlds that point the way to change. Bloch attempted to teach hope by writing twenty-one hundred pages describing the utopias of humanity, a testimony to the universality of imaginary worlds. It can be quite boring to read through such a heap of utopias, but the wave of hope that carried him away does not leave us unaffected when we read it; our emotion feeds on a longing for the impossible and the creative.

Hope for Bloch was akin to inspiration and creativity. Disappointment results from not understanding that utopias must not be made wholly real. Utopias are lamps hidden in the darkness, as Bloch pointed out. This definition can lead to an understanding of hope as a form of revolt. We can learn to hope by revolting against bad experiences: "Against my better judgment I am going to take the risk of thinking the impossible, and hope for something better." The success of Solidarity in Poland is an example of hope leading to something better. We resist the idea that things have always been as they are, or always have to be, and that everything falls apart in the end anyway. The word "resistance" has many overtones in French. Hope can also be a matter of decision. But hope has no power of resistance if it is a simple denial of hopelessness in which we tell ourselves that "things generally turn out as well as they can." The revolt begins when we say, "Yes, things often turn out badly, and yet I am foolish enough to think that they may improve. *How could* things be better?"

Asking how things could be better marks the onset of qualified dissatisfaction. Bloch's well-informed hope is no repression of the darker side of life. Earlier we said that hope is patient in contrast to expectation. Bloch's hope, close to longing and expectation, is not very patient.

How do we reach absolute hope? Bollnow wrote that there are situations in which we suddenly have the sense that the future is open. We can experience this as a threat or as a sustaining ground. Since openness to the future is frightening, it represents a huge challenge. Think for a moment of a few things that you cherish and have come to expect, and then imagine that the future is open to any change. You may find yourself trembling. Basic trust plays its part here. Although we are not normally conscious of it, basic trust — trust in ourselves and others, trust in life — underlies and supports active hope. As long as things are going relatively well, we have concrete hopes filled with images and ideas. When we collapse in a heap of shattered hopes, we may still be sustained by a hope that is absolute and devoid of images. Gone are any definite ideas about the future; only a sense of being carried and sustained remains. This is why Bollnow speaks of hope delivering us to a new sense of safety and security, of *Geborgenheit*.

I would like to offer an example. I once gave a seminar on human crises in which I attempted to find out how many of the participants had experienced a creative leap out of a dead-end situation into a situation of new promise. Such a leap would be related to the transition from anxiety to hope. A woman between the age of thirty and forty told about her experience: She had had two automobile accidents that had intimidated her and left her convinced that she would have to watch every step from now on if she wanted to stay alive. She found this way of being completely intolerable. One day she said to herself, "Why am I hanging on so desperately to life? There's no point in it," after which she let go of herself, expecting to die. To her surprise, she felt carried. "It was a joy to hope," she reported. "I had no idea what the future would bring, but I just felt carried and filled with hope." Her body was still suffering from severe injuries. The task remaining would have been to transform her experience of absolute hope into concrete hope.

I see hope as the basis for inspiration, creativity, and joy because it contains the dimension of basic trust. Archetypal images that express joy, inspiration, and hope also express basic trust. At the beginning of this book, I presented a view of emotion as existential involvement communicated to other persons in the form of signals that have an outer, physical side as well as an inner, unconscious side and can be expressed in archetypal images. I spoke of joy as a meaningful coincidence of the ego and the Self in the anticipation of something unexpected. The archetypal image of this emotion would be the motif of waiting for the arrival of the divine child. The experience of harmony in the anticipation of something more has elsewhere been described as the process of individuation. I referred to Dionysus as an archetypal image of inspiration. The archetype of the divine child can take many forms; Dionysus is a form that emphasizes the aspects of unanticipated newness and indestructibility. Joy is not indestructible; it can be killed. Dionysus suggests eternal transformation through vitality. It is clear that a mother belongs here, too—mother goddesses, feminine goddesses. There is no divine child without a mother.

The emotion of hope, like inspiration, has roots in the archetype of the divine child. In hope, the qualities of indestructibility, discord, and revolt are secondary to the qualities of generational growth, action, and redemption. For example, Jesus represents the archetype of the divine child that expresses the qualities of life associated with hope: "But we hope he will redeem Israel." Again, Jesus should be seen in relation to his mother, Mary, as the Catholic Church wisely recognizes. With each of the many variations on the motif of the divine child, we find a mother complex and a mother archetype. I see hope as belonging primarily—though not exclusively—to the realm of the mother archetype viewed as the foundation of life and vitality, which induces feelings of *Geborgenheit,* fullness, and assurance that the necessities of life will be provided. Also associated with this archetype are feelings of oneness with other persons and with the cosmos.

The argument of this book could be summarized by saying that we are not only flung into life, as the emotion of anxiety suggests, but we are also carried by life. We have been asking

whether transformation also takes place when we surrender ourselves to the elated emotions, and I have attempted to provide
an answer. Transformation takes place in both cases, through
anxiety as well as through joy; the question is only where does
each lead? Through the elated emotions we find symbiosis, and
our ego boundaries are not so defined. Yet by experiencing more
fullness, we gather strength and paradoxically become more autonomous. We experience being carried and sustained, and we
experience self-existence by forgetting ourselves rather than by
fighting for ourselves. We enjoy vitality, the richness of the
discoverable. This is a form of transformation that is based on
the realm of the mother archetype, in contrast to that based
on the father archetype, where we reflect on our difficulties in
order to become conscious of them. Individuation in this context has much more to do with separation.

We have dealt at length with problems associated with joy
and symbiosis: boundlessness, overlooking the balance between
height and breadth, becoming "high flown," and losing touch
with reality. We have also asked whether the emotions of elation can be learned, communicated, or stimulated.

Biogenetics tells us that our capacity for joy and hope is
predetermined. Depth psychology offers a different view. I myself think we can be infected by the elated emotions. Recollection offers one way to learn joy. Through the biographical reconstruction of joy, we can "reinfect" ourselves by dipping into
past joys and allowing them to rise again. Unfortunately this
is not so easy to accomplish with inspiration and hope. We experience inspiration and hope much later in life than joy, and
they are less common than joy, as well. However, it should be
possible to recall situations in which we were inspired or were
inspiring, and perhaps also situations in which hope came
through. We have found that there are infectious texts, inspiring imaginary worlds, and perhaps above all, music. Music and

dance are extremely conducive to infectious joy. I always say that one should really dance and not just talk about dancing. If you had experienced this book in its original form—as lectures—you would have spent the last few minutes with me listening to Beethoven's "Ode to Joy," which was a musical rendition of Schiller's poem "Freude schöner Götterfunken" (Joy of Divine Sparks): "Wir betreten feuertrunken himmlisch Dein Heiligentum" (Drunken with fire, we enter your holy shrine). Perhaps the most important line is "Alle Menschen werden Brüder. Seid umschlungen Millionen diesen Kuss der ganzen Welt" (All humanity becomes one family. May millions of these kisses embrace the world).

The emotions of elation must not be regarded as secondary or lowered to the status of ornaments; they are essential in their own right. The isolation produced by anxiety is one-sided without the alliance created by joy. If we are able to see joy, inspiration, and hope as sharing the same level of importance as anxiety and grief, those around us will not remain unaffected. We should not be ashamed of our delight. It would be an odd thing to be ashamed of plenty and not of poverty.

Epilogue

IT IS IMPORTANT that we human beings feel our wounds and know our inhibitions, the places where we are blocked. To know our difficult sides, which often make us what we are, we must be able to understand and accept the story of our suffering and misfortune.

But it is just as important to know our strengths, to see the oases of happiness where they appear in the landscape of our life stories, and to give due weight to our capacity, in spite of everything, to take deep delight. Otherwise we carry around a one-sided image of ourselves that locks us in the position of victims: victims of our parents and of life. But we are not simply victims; life has its successes and joys for us, too. Our oases of happiness give us the strength both to face our difficulties realistically and to realize how we perpetuate the bad experiences we have suffered by recreating them for those around us.

Individuation means becoming an individual person, one who is separated from one's parents to a degree appropriate to one's age, and who is differentiated from one's projected parental complexes as well. Individuation also means becoming increasingly oneself and increasingly whole. The concept of individuation clearly draws on the idea of emancipation: we should be ruled neither from within nor from without if we are to become more autonomous, more individual. Even if Jung says that relationship to oneself is at once relationship to other human beings [Jung, vol. 16, par. #445], I still think that connectedness to other persons, which goes far beyond stereotypical ways of relating as defined by traditional marriage and societal roles, receives too little attention in the concept of individuation as it stands.

The process of individuation takes on its fullest potential and significance only when we are able to undergo repeated experiences of symbiotic fusion with other persons, thus creating the emotional basis for solidarity and fellowship. It seems to me that the elated emotions give us access to this aspect of the individuation process.

These symbiotic connections are not to be seen as merely a kind of generosity, an ability to put aside our own interests when we feel taken care of within an enlarged context of relationship. Symbiotic connectedness conveys a genuine feeling of *Geborgenheit* (safe, secure, protected). Elated feelings give us the experience of feeling sustained and carried in life, an experience we call hope — hope in the unforeseen, hope for the better, for newness and change. This hope carries us with it, allowing us to bear much of what we often think is unbearable.

Geborgenheit, which arises especially when joy and inspiration are shared with others, has an important social dimension: it allows us to approach each other with a transformed attitude. Freed of our constant fear of attack, slander, and harm, we are less apt to erect barriers, and more apt to build bridges. The experience of being able to construct something together with others affords still more joy and heightens our sense of standing within an interlocking web, a web that supports mutual dependence in a positive sense: I do not always have to construct everything completely by myself. And I witness how my initiative has a ripple effect that transcends my own efforts, returning to affect me in new ways. In enthusiasm, ego boundaries are loosened so that ideas stemming from the unconscious reach me more readily, and at the same time the reception of these ideas is modified by the influence of other persons, who are less distanced from me.

In this form of inspiration the question is less what my unconscious wants from me, and more what the communal unconscious, or even the collective unconscious in the Jungian sense, has to contribute to the contemporary situation, not only for the self-regulation of the individual psyche, but for the self-regulation of psychic dynamics appearing in larger groups of people facing important existential issues to which they deliberately make themselves vulnerable. This impulse for self-regulation can only be taken up and passed on by persons who are emotionally involved, who allow themselves to be gripped by a problem, and who can move themselves to act—in other words, persons who can let themselves get enthusiastic about the search for the solution to a problem, and who, amidst their enthusiasm, are still capable of communicating their ideas to each other and of translating them into practical measures. Inspiration and enthusiasm then function as a uniting principle that lays an effective foundation for creative change, whether in a small circle, the family, a working team, or even entire nations and the world.

Obviously enthusiasm is not always effective; it cools off, allowing routine to step into its place as a uniting principle. This may provide the occasion for more sober reflection, where scrutiny of concepts goes hand in hand with the erection of barriers between us. Under these circumstances it is much more difficult to organize major creative projects. We are much more familiar with the phase of reflective sobriety than we are with that of passionate inspiration. A time of sobriety is also necessary, but it is important to return ever again to a time of inspiration. Those who know the special connectedness with other persons that arises out of shared joy and enthusiasm for a common project—whose involvement is emotional rather than strategic, who know the feeling of being carried and sustained that comes of shared joy—will, even in times of increased separateness and need for clarity, have a longing for the existential feeling of connectedness and will want to avail themselves of their right to it.

We must become conscious of how important the elated emotions really are for our lives and for the life of communities and of society. Bound together in their deepest cores, joy, inspiration, and hope strengthen each other. Joy is the most common, everyday emotion of the three, and is thus the most readily accessible; it comes when we allow it into our lives directly, or indirectly—through memory or in the company of children or other persons. Joy is an emotion that wants to be shared. As joy multiplies, it opens doors to inspiration and hope, puts us on the far side of divisiveness by focusing our attention on what we share, and delivers us the energy we need to realize our common ground.

Glossary

active imagination. The process by which a strong but flexible ego complex allows intangible unconscious material (complexes, dreams, and images) to be expressed in a tangible product such as painting, poetry, or song.

affects. More primary than feelings, affects are emotions that shoot through a person with an intensity that provokes a physical reaction and usually a social reaction as well.

animus. An archetypal masculine figure contrasted with the archetypal feminine figure, the anima. Fascinating animus figures appear in the dreams, fantasies, and projections of women and men, for example in the guise of the mysterious stranger, the divine youth, the fascinating thinker, the lightning-quick divinity, the mysterious, christlike man, and so forth. In a survey I conducted among colleagues, the emotional quality most often used to describe a constellated animus was "mentally or spiritually gripped," followed by "inner trembling," "moved by desire," "searching for the connections between things," and "fascination with words." The emotion associated with the animus moves us to grasp, or to want to grasp, "what makes the world cohere in its innermost core," to penetrate a matter, to come to a solution, "to smite the fire out of things, the fire out of fire itself."

The spatial dimension assigned to the animus is unequivocally vertical.

archetype. Anthropological constants on the planes of experiencing, imaging, processing, and behaving. Archetypes regulate, modify, and motivate the mind's conscious contents. They are expressions of the human condition and of human being that cause us in given situations to experience typical images, emotions, instincts, and physical reactions. Archetypal ideas and events experienced consciously must be distinguished from the archetypes themselves, which are basic forms characterized by particular formal elements and fundamental meanings that can be only approximately comprehended. These archetypal ideas are moreover always mediated through our personal complexes, which explains why in archetypal situations a great deal of personal material is interwoven with matter that is typical. The archetype is thus in part a structuring factor in the psychic and physical realm. An archetype possesses a very specific dynamic. This dynamic functions to bring something from potentiality into actuality, to create a constellation, to make us feel something like instinctual energy.

collective unconscious. Jung distinguished between the collective unconscious, whose structural elements are the archetypes, and the personal unconscious, whose structural elements are above all the feeling-toned complexes composed of repressed experiences, which are capable of becoming conscious. According to Jung, the collective unconscious, being identical in everyone, forms a common, transpersonal psychic ground.

communal unconscious. A mysterious relationship or fusion appears to exist between the unconscious of the analyst and that of the analysand. This shared unconscious is sensed as the atmosphere of the relationship, and it can explain why a psychic "infection" is possible, in which, for example, the analyst feels in his or her body the unperceived and unexpressed anxiety of the analysand. This unconscious relationship is the prerequisite for "countertransference" and when this is functioning at its best provides the basis by which the analysand can take advantage of the analyst's self-regulation.

complex. An emotionally charged, autonomous or split-off personality—like part of one's own psyche and self—that is related to personal traumatic conflicts and archetypal themes and issues.

ego. The center of one's consciousness and conscious identity.

ego complex. Themes associated with the ego complex revolve around the issues of identity, the development of identity, and the self-esteem connected with them. The basis of our identity is the feeling of vitality, which is closely associated with the feeling of ego activity. It is the feeling of being alive, and rooted in this feeling lies the ego's chance to mobilize itself actively in life and finally to realize itself. Vitality, ego activity, and self-realization are mutually dependent. The ego complex has, like every complex, an archetypal core, namely, the Self in the Jungian sense. (In the Freudian tradition, the ego complex is called the self.) The Self is understood here as the center and totality of the personality as it has become and will become in the future. The Self yields up in the course of a lifetime our hidden life goal through the development of the ego complex as the Self intended it to be. This means that the ego complex's process of becoming conscious should be viewed dynamically: ever new constellations are to be expected in the course of a lifetime, related to the phases and stages described by developmental psychology. A completely unique individuation process overlies this typical course of life-span events that has to do with our fully individual life possibilities and our private encounters with formative situations. As with every complex, the ego complex comprises a theme of development and a theme of inhibition. On the side of development would be the increase of autonomy in self-realization, self-expression, the growth of self-consciousness, the ability to practice self-preservation, take risks, and to enter increasingly into relationship with one's self. On the side of inhibition would be the issue of heteronomy, being conditioned from the outside by social structures and concrete human relationships, and from the inside by complexes that are split off from consciousness.

ego functions. Functions that we not only ascribe to the ego but may even assume to be identical with the ego and which give us the means to perceive and observe our ego complex, to develop consciousness of ourselves, and to systematize the world of consciousness in general. Thus these functions give us the means to orient ourselves, to know what is outer and what is inner, to differentiate ego from non-ego, to perceive the reactions of our fellows and to adjust our behavior accordingly. The names given to the primary autonomous ego functions are: capacity for perception, sensation, memory, thinking, conceptual formation, spatial and temporal orientation, orientation with regard to one's own person, attention, motor activity, and even defense mechanisms. These ego functions can be sufficiently functional, or they can be deficient in various ways.

emotion. The inclusive term covering feeling, affect, and mood.

feeling. An emotion that can be perceived and named, accompanied by images that can be communicated. It has definite causes and goals.

individuation. The life-long process toward wholeness, individuality, differentiation from one's parents, parental complexes, and projections.

mood. The emotional state or attunement of a person's being.

psyche. Originally this meant soul, but it has come to mean the entirety of one's mind, which includes conscious and unconscious components, including the soul.

Self. The center and totality of the psyche, the person, and the world. It is very close to the concept of a Supreme Being inside and outside the individual. This is in distinction to the "self" (small s), which is identical with the ego complex.

symbiosis. Fusion with another. Ideally fusion is only momentary; otherwise it can lead to extreme dependency.

transcendence. Involves overcoming the division of conscious (ego) and unconscious, usually by a feeling such as love or an archetypal symbol that unifies and contains the tension of opposites.

References

Anderson, C. M. 1974. *Joy beyond Grief.* Grand Rapids: Zondervan.

Anderson, H. H. 1959. *Creativity and Its Cultivation.* New York: Harper and Row.

Bachmann, I. 1971. *Malina.* Frankfurt: Suhrkamp.

Binswanger, L. 1955. "Über die manische Lebensform" in *Ausgewählte Vorträge und Aufsätze,* vol. II. Bern: Francke.

Bleuler, E. 1966. *Lehrbuch der Psychiatrie.* Berlin: Springer.

Bloch, E. 1959. *Das Prinzip Hoffnung.* Frankfurt: Suhrkamp.

Bollnow, O. F. 1956. *Das Wesen der Stimmungen.* Frankfurt: Rostermann.

————. 1955, 1979. *Neue Geborgenheit: Das Problem einer Überwindung des Existentialismus.* Stuttgart: Kohlhammer.

Camus, A. 1955. *The Myth of Sisyphus.* New York: Random House.

Czikszentmihalyi, M. 1975. *Beyond Boredom and Anxiety: The Experience of Play in Work and Games.* San Francisco: Jossey-Bass.

Datan, N., and L. H. Ginsberg, eds. 1975. *Life-Span Developmental Psychology: Normative Life Crises.* New York: Academic Press.

Eliade, M. 1978. *A History of Religious Ideas.* Chicago: University of Chicago Press.

Ellul, J. 1973. *Hope in Time of Abandonment.* Trans. C. E. Hopkin. New York: Seabury.

Erikson, E. 1959. *Identity and the Life Cycle.* New York: International Universities Press.

Euripides, *The Bacchae,* in D. Grene and R. Lattimore, eds. 1959,

1960. *The Complete Greek Tragedies.* Chicago: University of Chicago Press.

Frisch, M. 1972. *Tagebuch 1946–1949.* Frankfurt: Suhrkamp.

Fromm, E. 1964. *The Heart of Man: Its Genius for Good and Evil.* New York: Harper and Row.

Henseler, H. 1974, 1980. *Narzisstische Krisen: Zur Psychodynamik des Selbstmords.* Reinbek: Rowohlt.

Izard, C. E. 1977. *Human Emotions.* New York: Harper and Row.

Jaspers, K. 1965. *Allgemeine Psychopathologie.* Berlin: Springer.

Jung, C. G. 1921. *Psychological Types.* In *The Collected Works,* vol. 6. Princeton: Princeton University Press.

———. 1946. *The Psychology of the Transference.* In *Collected Works,* vol. 16. Princeton: Princeton University Press.

———. 1955, 1956. *Mysterium Coniunctionis.* In *The Collected Works,* vol. 14. Princeton: Princeton University Press.

Kahl, G., ed. 1981. *Logik des Herzens: Die Soziale Dimension der Gefühle.* Frankfurt: Suhrkamp.

Kast, V. 1980. *Das Assoziationsexperiment in der therapeutischen Praxis.* Stuttgart: Bonz.

———. 1986a. *The Nature of Loving: Patterns of Human Relationship.* Trans. Boris Matthews. Wilmette, Ill.: Chiron Publications.

———. 1986b. *Sisyphos: Der Alte Stein — Der neue Weg.* Stuttgart: Kreuz.

———. 1988. *A Time to Mourn: Growing through the Grief Process.* Einsiedeln: Daimon.

———. 1990a. *The Creative Leap.* Wilmette, Ill.: Chiron Publications.

———. 1990b. *Die Dynamik der Symbole: Grundlagen der Jung'schen Psychotherapie.* Olten: Walter.

Kerényi, K. 1976. *Dionysus: Archetypal Image of Indestructible Life.* Princeton: Princeton University Press.

Koestler, A. 1964. *The Act of Creation.* London: Hutchinson.

Kretschmer, E. 1951. *Körperbau und Charakter.* Berlin: Springer.

Landau, E. 1984. *Kreatives Erleben.* Munich: Reinhardt.

Lersch, P. 1970. *Aufbau der Person.* Munich: Johann Ambrosius Barth.

Marcel, G. 1964. *Philosophie der Hoffnung.* Munich: List.

Maslow, A. 1962. "Emotional Blocks to Creativity." In *A Source Book for Creative Thinking*, ed. S. Parnes and H. Harding. New York: Charles Scribner's Sons.

May, I. 1853. "The Nature of Creativity." In H. Anderson, ed., *Creativity and Its Cultivation*. New York: Harper and Row.

Moser, U. 1978. "Affektsignal und aggressives Verhalten." *Psyche* 32: 229–58.

Nablowsky, I. 1889. *Das Gefühlsleben*. Leipzig: Reclam.

Neumann, E. 1955. *The Great Mother*. Olten: Walter.

Nin, A. 1975. *A Woman Speaks*. Chicago: Swallow Press.

Nietzsche, F. 1956. *The Birth of Tragedy*. New York: Doubleday.

Plügge, H. 1954. "Über die Hoffnung." In Plügge, ed., *Wohlbefinden und Missbefinden*. Tübingen: Mohr.

Otto, W. F. 1981. *Dionysus: Myth and Cult*. Dallas: Spring.

Rosner, S., and L. Abt. 1972. *The Creative Experience*. New York: Delta.

Sartre, Jean Paul. 1946. *L'existentialisme est un humanisme*. Paris: Nagel.

Scheler, N. 1983. *Die Stellung des Menschen im Kosmos*. 10th edition. Bern: Francke.

Schutz, W. 1967. *Joy: Expanding Human Awareness*. New York: Grove.

Taylor, C., ed. 1964. *Creativity: Progress and Potential*. New York: McGraw Hill.

Tölle, R. 1986. *Psychiatrie*. Berlin: Springer.

Ulich, D. 1982. *Das Gefühl*. Munich: Urban, Schwarzenberg.

von Uexküll, T., and W. Wesiack. 1986. "Wissenschaftstheorie und psychosomatische Medizin, ein bio-psycho-soziales Modell." In von Uexküll, ed., *Psychosomatische Medizin*. Munich: Urban and Schwarzenberg.

von Uslar, D. 1987. *Grundfragen der Psychologie: Das Bild des Menschen in der Psychologie*. Stuttgart: Hirzel.

Ziegler, T. 1912. *Das Gefühl*. Berlin: Göschen'sche Verlagsbuchhandlung.

Index

social environment: of emotions,
13
socialization: of joy, 76–81
social order: ecstasy and, 121, 122;
women and, 121, 124, 125
solidarity. *See* affiliation: relatedness; symbiosis
soul: and nature, xiii; emotions related to, xi; in psychology, x
stress factors, 62
suicide, 136
surrender, 110
symbiosis, 7, 154, 155, 156, 165; and
development, 129; and ecstasy,
127, 130; and individuation, 129,
158; with nature, 125, 126, 127;
sadism and, 90, 91
symbols, 151; Dionysian, 6, 115, 116,
120, 123
synchronicity, x

temperament, 24–25; and mania,
100; swings in, 25, 26–27
Teresa of Avila, 128
therapy: and affect, 13; and emotions, 12; goals of, 15; and hope,
138; joy and, 4–5, 7, 20; tech-
niques of, 4, 110, 129
Tölle, R., 101
tragedy, 119
transcendence, 43, 47, 139, 165
transformation, 4, 20, 43; Dionysus and, 123, 154; elated emotions and, 108, 123, 155; need for,
108
transitions, 63, 153
transpersonal Self, 6, 7. *See also*
Self

trust, 137; in self, 45
Tutu, Desmond, xiii

unconscious, 6, 94, 121, 159, 162;
and creativity, 109, 110; and ego,
128–29; and hope, 137; and inspiration, 109, 110; and longing, 145;
and vision, 137
unity, 127, 128. *See also* symbiosis
universal hope. *See* absolute hope
unus mundus, 127
utopias, 113, 151–52

variety: and interest, 77
vegetation: ceremony of, 121; god
of, 116–17
vision, 113, 119, 124, 129, 139; and
hope, 136, 138, 148; and illusion,
contrasted, 149, 151; for life, 137
von Droste-Hülshoff, Annette, 147,
149
von Uslar, D., 21

warmth, 71, 112
wholeness, 127, 137, 157
will to live, 136
wine, 118, 119
wine god, 116
wishes, 145
Woman Speaks, A (Nin), 68–69
womb, 127
women: and Dionysian mystery,
121, 122, 123, 124, 125, 131
Wordsworth, William, xiii
work, 142; as source of joy, 49; and
mania, 106

Zeus, 117

Joy, Inspiration, and Hope was composed into type on a Compu-graphic digital phototypesetter in twelve point Bembo with two points of spacing between the lines. Bembo was also selected for display. The book was designed by Jim Billingsley, typeset by Metricomp, Inc., printed offset by Thomson-Shore, Inc., and bound by John H. Dekker & Sons, Inc. The paper on which this book is printed carries acid-free characteristics for an effective life of at least three hundred years.

TEXAS A&M UNIVERSITY PRESS
College Station